# DELINQUENCY AND CHILD GUIDANCE

*Selected Papers*

AUGUST AICHHORN

*Menninger Clinic Monograph Series, No. 15*

# DELINQUENCY AND CHILD GUIDANCE

## Selected Papers

*by*

## AUGUST AICHHORN

*Edited by*

OTTO FLEISCHMANN, PAUL KRAMER, and HELEN ROSS

INTERNATIONAL UNIVERSITIES PRESS, INC.
New York                                    New York

# Contents

# Foreword

It is not unusual for the reading public to identify an author
with his *magnum opus* only, as it has happened with regard
to August Aichhorn and his *Wayward Youth*. But even if this
unique book contains Aichhorn's most brilliant and original
conceptions set out in the most concise and pleasing form,
there remain still sidelines to his efforts which workers following his lead cannot afford to ignore. Leading up to his
main publication or branching out from it, Aichhorn has
given evidence of the laborious ways and means by which his
insights were acquired and made excursions into new fields
which he attempted to conquer for psychoanalytic thinking.
Not all the hopes which he entertained for the increased
understanding and handling of delinquents were realized
under the restricted external conditions and with the groping knowledge available to him in his lifetime. Nevertheless,
as pioneering thinkers do, in his daily work, his addresses
and essays, he set forth suggestions and opened up lines of
reasoning which deserve to be placed before the public and
are apt to stimulate further thought and action in his
followers.

ANNA FREUD

7

# Introduction

Since the publication of *Wayward Youth,* a translation of *Verwahrloste Jugend* (1925), the name of August Aichhorn requires little introduction to workers in the field of juvenile delinquency. The ideas and principles described by Aichhorn with deceptive simplicity in that classical book have permeated the thinking of professional workers in the field and have encouraged emulation and stimulated independent and original work along the lines pioneered by him. The boldness of his ideas, his radical departure from both the punitive and the charitable but ignorant attitude toward youthful offenders, and the substitution of an approach based on dynamic understanding of the causes of delinquency and of the needs of the delinquents have remained unequaled, as has the consistency with which he applied his principles and his insight in institutional treatment and in his work with countless children and parents in trouble.

The selection of essays offered in this volume to the American reader continues and extends the ideas presented in *Wayward Youth.* To mention but a few of Aichhorn's fundamental views, he considers delinquency a condition the beginnings of which reach into the past long before the appearance of actual symptoms. This latent stage of delinquency represents the true pathology in contrast to its later manifest symptoms, which are often mistakenly viewed as the essence of delinquent behavior. The early personality changes represented in latent delinquency are results of disturbances within the personality structure, a disturbance for which neglect of the child's fundamental needs for love and tenderness is largely if not wholly responsible. This neglect may spring from depriving the child of his legitimate needs or from overwhelming him with a flood of affection which he is unable to tolerate. Faulty and deficient superego development is regularly found in wayward and delinquent children. This defect is most often caused by the parents' failure to meet the child's primary need for affection, by the child's identification with latent or manifest superego defects in the parents, by conflicting identifications with disunited parental figures, by contradictory demands imposed on the child, and a variety of other factors, which Aichhorn illuminates with clinical examples in the text.

The delinquent child's family lives in a libidinal equilibrium which is maintained at the expense of the child. The outbreak of delinquent behavior is often the expression of the child's protest against this state of affairs or of his inability to bear the burden further. The psychoanalytic concepts of ego, superego, and id were vivid and living entities to Aichhorn and he, perhaps more than most psychoanalysts, used them in his work, observed their operation, and was concerned with their dynamic interdependence. Aichhorn was engaged in a deliberate and carefully planned amelioration of the disturbed relations between ego, superego, and id, and with the restoration of a proper balance between the forces represented by them. In this he was singularly successful. The large variety of manifestations of delinquency is to be seen as a scale of variations in the interplay of psychic forces represented by the different personality structures. Delineation of the dynamic and economic position of delinquency in relation to neuroses and psychoses was first attempted by Aichhorn and occupied his interest to the end of his life. The society in which the delinquent finds himself provides the external forms, and the individual intrapersonal conflict the essential content of the delinquency. Aichhorn did not differentiate as sharply as present American authors do between "sociologic" and "individual" delinquents.[1]

It may come as a surprise to some that Aichhorn was as ready and capable of using firmness and force in his approach to the delinquent and to his family as he was of showing them kindness and inexhaustible patience. There was an utter absence of sentimentality in the man and in his work; instead there was a calm weighing of the forces at play and a deliberate use of conflict and powerful emotion for the purpose of the re-education of the delinquent. He considered the creation of a relationship of complete confidence and of an intense emotional attachment to the worker a *sine qua non* of all efforts at re-education. In psychoanalytic terms, all rehabilitation must begin with the establishment of a strong, positive transference; success is impossible without it. The papers give a vivid picture of Aichhorn's unmatched skill in this regard. A particularly striking example is given in Aichhorn's description of the creation and utilization of the "narcissistic transference" in the treatment of the juvenile impostor—an accomplishment of great practical and theoretical significance.

The reader will find in the last paper an expression of Aichhorn's views on the subject of the personality features desirable in those who work with youthful delinquents. It should be added that Aichhorn always stressed the indispensable requirement that the worker be thoroughly familiar with the social "milieu" of the child under his care. Aichhorn possessed an amazingly comprehensive and detailed knowledge of the mores, customs, and standards, i.e., of the "total

[1] For an appreciation of Aichhorn's influence on American child psychiatrists and child guidance workers see Adelaide Johnson (1959), Juvenile Delinquency. In: *American Handbook of Psychiatry*, ed. S. Arieti. New York: Basic Books.

culture," of the different social groups and subgroups in Vienna from which his charges came. The majority were from the laboring and lower-middle classes, but many derived from Vienna's wealthier circles. From the late 20s an increasing number of people from central and eastern Europe sought Aichhorn's help.

Aichhorn's personality and the unique manner of his work received perceptive and imaginative evaluation by a number of his students and friends. The reader's attention is called particularly to Anna Freud's obituary notice (1951) and to K. R. Eissler's biographical outline introducing the volume, *Searchlights on Delinquency,* dedicated to Aichhorn on the occasion of his 70th birthday.[2] The present writer can but confirm the accuracy of these authors' description of Aichhorn's personality and his superb work, and add with some regret the personal observation that to one who had the privilege of listening to Aichhorn and observing him at work, the reading of his papers is at first somewhat disappointing, almost anticlimactic.

Virtually all of the papers presented here were read by Aichhorn to lay audiences and not prepared for publication. Inevitably the color and vitality of his presentation and the immediacy of the relationship which he most skillfully established with his audience are lost in the printed version. The sometimes circumstantial introductory remarks which Aichhorn was wont to present in a slow and deliberate fashion while calmly scanning the audience before him might tend to appear superfluous or contrived in print, but they were a vital element of Aichhorn's presentation. He used these first few minutes to establish a positive rapport with his audience, thus making them receptive to his ideas.

[2] Freud, A. (1951), Obituary: August Aichhorn. *International Journal of Psycho-Analysis,* 32:51-56. Eissler, K. R. (1949), A Biographical Outline. In: *Searchlights on Delinquency.* New York: International Universities Press.

The main task of collecting the essays in the present volume, dispersed as they were in various periodicals difficult to obtain, was accomplished by the late Dr. Otto Fleischmann. He arranged the first version of the translation of these essays, a labor hard to overestimate. Dr. Adolphe Gourevitch originally translated the first six essays in this volume, Mrs. Gerda Frank the seventh. Dr. Fleischmann was fortunate in receiving the help of Aichhorn's widow and of his devoted secretaries, Miss E. Skopnik and Miss R. Dworschak, who supplied him with manuscripts in their possession and with much relevant information. Particular acknowledgement is due the Menninger Foundation whose material help made the translation of this work possible and who have elected to publish this volume as a monograph in the Menninger Foundation Monograph Series. Dr. Otto Fleischmann's untimely death prevented him from completing his task. Helen Ross, who has once before rendered distinguished service to Aichhorn's work, as one of the translators and editors of *Wayward Youth*, provided invaluable help by reviewing the whole material, revising the translation, and adding explanatory editorial remarks.

P.K.

# I

# On Education in Training Schools

Though the official term is "correctional education," I am intentionally speaking of education *(Erziehung)* for two reasons. First, "correctional education" may mislead one to believe that we are dealing with an education which is enforced on the pupil, and, indeed, one hears much about compulsory measures current in reformatories. Correctional education seems to be a process carried out against the will of those who are liable to it. Second, my choice of words delimits the subject more sharply, as against the work of youth welfare agencies and the training attempted within the independent youth movements.

Between the upbringing of normal children and the re-education of wayward youth there certainly exists a deep and intimate relationship. Nevertheless, in our training schools, we are still far from being able to draw definite conclusions which would be applicable to the upbringing of the normal child. Among our charges we find borderline cases that verge upon neurosis and psychosis, and bring us

Lecture delivered at the Viennese Psychoanalytical Society on June 21, 1922; first published as "Über die Erziehung in Besserungsanstalten" [Education in Reform Schools]. *Imago*, 9:189-221, 1923.

therefore into actual contact with psychiatry; on the other
hand, we find cases that come close to, or merge with the
normal child, so that our work has some kinship with the
guidance provided by youth welfare organizations and by
independent youth movements.

In all the children and youths entrusted to our care, in the
institution of Ober-Hollabrunn as well as that of St. Andrä,[1]
we were able to recognize the existence of a factor of release, whatever the various, deeper-seated causes of delinquency. In order to recover from the blows which social life
inflicts upon them, human beings need a haven of peace,
which is normally provided in the family. When the individual has such a haven, his instinctual life is able to manifest
itself within socially acceptable limits. But if he lacks this
refuge, his mental equilibrium, which is never entirely stable,
becomes more easily disturbed, and, given the appropriate
disposition, delinquency results.

The task of institutions for delinquent youth should be to
remove the permanent effects of such disturbances in the
mental equilibrium. The ways of influencing a delinquent
child must differ substantially from the usual education of
normal children. Our work has much in common with that
of the psychiatrist, and we should perhaps describe it as
*treatment* rather than education.

We do not share the opinion of those who believe that the
child's later development is entirely determined by his hered-
ity. We stand here on the firm ground of psychoanalysis: the
character and intensity of a child's libidinal bond to the
persons of his earliest environment are among the determining factors of his later life. This is entirely borne out by our
not inconsiderable success in the rehabilitation of many
delinquents, a success which we owe to the influence we
exercise upon the libido's development toward sublimation
and compensation. What we mean is best shown by two

---

[1] In December 1918, the City of Vienna established a Home for Viennese
Juvenile Delinquents in the former refugee camp at Ober-Hollabrunn; on
February 28, 1921, this Home was shifted to the former welfare institution
at St. Andrä.

cases, one of a seventeen-year-old homosexual, the other a sixteen-year-old boy described by our consultant psychiatrist, Dr. Lazar, as mildly schizoid.

The sixteen-year-old was a youth from a good family of the upper-middle class; he was sent to our training school because of repeated stealing at home. Having failed to improve at several other correctional institutions, he was entrusted to our care. How bad his thieving was can be judged by his father's statement: "The boy would have caused our ruin if he had stayed at home any longer." He was extremely irritable and difficult to handle. At times he imagined that other boys wanted to attack him, and he assaulted his companions, or even his own counselor and other persons of his environment. After a while, he took revenge upon our superintendent, who he thought had slighted him. The very next night, he defecated at the door of the superintendent's apartment. Delusions of grandeur were expressed in the fantasy that he would become a leader of gangsters. Allegedly, he had formed his own gang in Vienna, and he imagined himself as its ruler. His father denied this fantasy altogether. The boy's behavior at our training school, and our repeated talks with him, confirmed the diagnosis made by our psychiatric consultant.

The youth was well developed in body but had less than normal intelligence. We took advantage of the highly aggressive and anal components of his character by providing him with an occupation in which he could achieve something physically without being exposed to unflattering comparison because of his deficient intelligence. In our school, we could offer him only the vegetable garden, where he could dig to his heart's content and busy himself with dung.

The seventeen-year-old boy was put to work in the tailor shop, where he learned in five months all that usually requires three years. The master tailor described him as a genius in his trade. During the entire period he was guilty of backsliding only once, when he tried to entice another pupil into homosexual practices.

In our opinion, successful vocational guidance in the case of this youth was achieved by taking a psychoanalytic attitude. We recognized the needs of his "libidinal economy," and helped him to find in eight hours of daily professional work the best prerequisite for automatic satisfaction of his psychological needs, in accordance with the pleasure principle (Freud, 1920).

Merely putting the boy to work in the tailor shop could not of course change the instinctual source from which he derived his psychic energy. But we recognized the dynamics of the libido components: we reckoned that his perverse libido would find an outlet in this particular, useful occupation, instead of bringing him into conflict with the police. It should be mentioned that the pupil had been placed in the tailor shop against his will, and that for several months he felt very uneasy. When, shortly before he left for a new institution at Eggenburg,[2] I happened to speak to him about his accomplishment in the shop, he replied with the voice of an enthusiastic tailor: "It's well, after all, if one is not always allowed to do as one wishes."

In both instances, a psychoanalytic approach—which distinguishes between a misused libido and its normal components usable in manual work—enabled us to employ vocational guidance as a means of successful re-education.

Complete psychoanalysis, notably in the first of the two cases, would have yielded more certain results. Obviously, for practical reasons, not every pupil in a training school can be subjected to such an analysis. However, we insist on having those pupils analyzed who are so difficult to handle as to be rejected by every group of inmates.[3]

[2] The training school at St. Andrä was being liquidated, because the City of Vienna was taking over from the Province of Lower Austria the big educational institution of Eggenburg (capacity 1,000 pupils) to which our pupils were transferred.

[3] Of course this will become possible only when the trained psychoanalyst is given his proper place within the framework of the reform institution. For the time being, we must take great pains in channeling toward serious study that psychoanalytic dilettantism which has broken out among the over-enthusiastic teachers.

Anyone who has occasion to visit reformatories of the old type is struck first of all by the sullen, reserved appearance of the pupils. He meets everywhere a cautious, suspicious attitude, with mistrustful glances full of hatred. Nobody looks him straight in the eye. That happy overflow of good cheer, which one expects in normal children, is entirely lacking. Whatever cheerfulness there is seems actually sad. Real spirits, real joy of life find a quite different expression. One shudders at the amount of hate pent up in these young people. Far from finding a release in the reformatory, this burden of hate seems only to grow heavier, as if stored for later explosion within society.

We had no idea of all this when we started our work at Ober-Hollabrunn. We were not burdened by any institutional traditions. We came from youth welfare organizations and from schools, without any previous training for our special task. We had perhaps some natural capacity for it, and certainly we felt much sympathy toward youth in general.

We perceived instinctively that we should first of all strive to bring some joy into the lives of these boys and girls, from fourteen to eighteen years of age. None among us considered them as juvenile delinquents, swindlers, or criminals, from whom society ought to be protected. To us they were human beings whom life had treated much too harshly; their negative attitude, or even their hatred of society, seemed not without some justification. It was up to us to create an environment wherein they could feel better. And the thing came to us quite naturally. Happy faces among the staff members, happiness welling up from the eyes of the children, laughter even among the eighteen-year-olds—for were not these merely our bigger kids? I still remember the tension with which we waited for our first ward, and how pleased he was when we fairly threw ourselves at him in order to "spoil" him. Later on, of course, we had to dispense with some of our initial exaggerations. But even our first boy was not at all harmed by the warmth we lavished upon him. He is today an assistant gardener in Vienna.

Thus we worked out—without knowing it, merely by creating a proper environment—what we may now term a practical psychology of reconciliation. We can say that this psychology is applicable in a vast majority of cases in training institutions.

We recognized very soon that the delinquent child is hungry for enjoyment, perhaps more sharply than the normal child. It is because of privation suffered in family and social life that these wayward young people seek satisfaction in delinquency.

It is our task to let our charges learn, through actual *experience*, that one may gain a much higher total amount of enjoyment in a life which is socially oriented.

I can sum up my entire judgment of "the institution" in one sentence: We must let the children experience at first hand that there is a higher sum total of pleasure in a socially directed life.

But if the pupils are really to experience anything, they must be brought into contact with the reality of living—not with a mere institution, which, however well-organized, remains alien to daily life. The less the environment in a training school resembles that of an "institution," the better: for otherwise the inmates will be withdrawn from actual life. The more the school conforms in character to a free community of people who enjoy living, the better are the prospects of rehabilitating the asocial child and of restoring him to normal social intercourse.

The great danger within the walls of an institution is that the pupil's individuality will fail to develop. There evolves all too easily a routine so that the pupil becomes a mere inmate with a number, in accordance with purely administrative requirements. Let us remind ourselves of our own childhood: what did it mean to us to have our own drawer, or cupboard, or box, or any other place that belonged to us alone, where we could hide our secrets from our parents, or from our brothers and sisters; a place which we might keep in good order, if it so pleased us, but which we could also leave in disorder, to our heart's content? How much of these early experiences is still effective in our later lives. But what happens in an "institution"? Everywhere the same order and style of living, enforced for the sake of uniformity. The reformatory's walls enclose the child on every side, cutting him off from life and forcing him into fantasies which are unhealthy, because they preclude any timely adjustment between desire and reality. How different it is when a youth lives in our institution.

Can we imagine that one who proved unable to bear the tyranny of social life would become rehabilitated through compulsory methods in a correctional institution? No, what the asocial child needs is an environment which gives him freedom of movement.

This was provided in Ober-Hollabrunn by assigning a separate bungalow to each group of pupils. In St. Andrä, on the other hand, the housing conditions were quite unfavorable. But the problem can be easily solved in every institution that has a number of cottages.

Upon admission to our training school our wayward children do not promptly surrender to the spell of their new surroundings. Some of them are merely astonished, incredulous, diffident. Many—those who have become inwardly tough, and are no longer able to yield to anything except brute force—see us simply as weaklings who do not dare tackle them. Still others, those who feel themselves on a higher level of intelligence, look down on us as dumb people to be outsmarted. Every attitude is represented, from brutish opposition to quiet scorn.

Because we know this, we do not try to win them over with words at the time of arrival. We place them in the so-called "In and Out" group, which comprises both newcomers and oldtimers. There the new inmates share the life of such pupils as are already fit for discharge from the training school. This offers the best conditions for a speedy adjustment of the newcomers to the school's environment. We gain also the advantage of being able to judge whether the pupils to be discharged are really capable of withstanding the strong pressure exercised by these new and still asocial elements in the group.

At the beginning, ethical values have no power of attraction. The young delinquent can be handled through his gross appetite for food. He wants an abundant diet, but does not care very much about its variety. The asocial child is not a gourmet. Yet he will never grasp that a teacher may be on his side and share his interests, so long as he gets cornmeal for supper while the teachers eat Hungarian goulash specially prepared for them. In training schools, it is a basic educational principle to have a single fare, cooked on the same stove and in the same pots. Difference in menu between pupils and teachers creates a strong feeling of distrust against the staff, a feeling which ultimately affects the entire relationship. The delinquent child will not trust the kind heart of the pedagogue!

We try to leave the pupils as free as possible. Timid people do not always recognize this necessity, and neighbors of an institution are apt to take it very badly. There is a great outcry when anything goes amiss, or when one of our inmates jumps a fence. But we are not to be led astray by any expressions of doubt, shock, or disapproval. As in psychoanalysis, the daily conflicts enable us to penetrate the innermost lives of our pupils and to grasp the unconscious motives of their actions.

Sometimes we have succeeded in bringing about a healing process of rehabilitation, either by frankly taking part in a pupil's acute conflict, or even by artificially paving the way for the outbreak of such a conflict. We have repeatedly prevented a pupil from running away—or, on the contrary (but please do not shudder)—we have provoked him into running away when it suited the needs of our teaching. It happens only seldom that a runaway deserts his institution because of a sudden impulse, or because of a dream; and in such cases it is difficult to prevent his desertion. Much more often, however, the impulse requires a period of maturation, lasting perhaps several days—which should not escape the trained eye of an attentive educator. Quite aside from our position against punishment of any kind in reform institutions, we consider it as an utter failure of pedagogic understanding when the statutes of a reformatory set it down as a rule that the returning runaway be punished with so many strokes of the rod. Desertion occurs when the "outer" world seems to be a more pleasurable place than the world "inside" the institution. If we succeed in having a talk with the pupil while he finds himself in the throes of this conflict, we can easily make the "inside" look more attractive than the "outside," even without alluding in any way to his intention of cutting loose. He will then renounce his intention, and stay at school. But another pupil, who wants to remain, can be talked just as easily into escaping from school, if we bring back the memory of the "outer" world in sufficiently pleasant colors.

I asked you not to be shocked at my statement about the occasional necessity of causing an inmate to run away. Of course this will not be a daily occurrence, only an exception. Such an instance follows:

We had a seventeen-year-old youth who was a gambler and a "man about town"; he had speculated on the stock exchange and had become a black-market operator. He had made a lot of money. His career started at the age of fifteen; he was a cashier, working for a street-corner "banker" or moneylender, who employed the clever and versatile boy as his agent in speculation, entrusting him with orders on the exchange and enabling him also to do business on his own. Thus the youth accumulated no less than 35,000 Austrian crowns, which made him independent. In 1917, it was quite a capital! The boy traveled to Galicia, purchasing foodstuffs and selling them on the black market in Vienna, a business which yielded high profits. In Vienna he led a dissolute life, haunting the night clubs, keeping women of doubtful morality, and playing cards with growing passion. The profits, and then the capital, dwindled and disappeared. In order to make a fresh start, he plundered his mother's linen chest. The mother, widowed after a most unhappy marriage, had repeatedly tried to steer her son into a better way of living. But as her efforts were all in vain, she finally applied for help to a youth welfare agency, which brought the young man to our training school.

He was one of those inmates who give no particular trouble as long as one is content with the externals of good conduct in an institution. Such boys are well behaved and obliging, often skillful and quite useful in simple office work. They know how to live and let live, and get along with their fellow pupils, among whom they may even assume a role of leadership. But when one comes to deal with them more closely, one encounters particular pedagogic difficulties. Inwardly corrupt, outwardly as smooth as eels, they offer no opening for any correctional influence. Their behavior is a mask, a good one, yet nothing but a mask. They do not follow the lead of their teacher, and thwart all his attempts at establishing a closer relationship with them. Transference, which must be especially strong if one hopes to achieve anything of educational value, is almost impossible to establish with such pupils. They are precisely those who never get into trouble in any institution, and soon convey the impression of having been cured. But once discharged and out on their own, they immediately revert to type. One is therefore never too cautious with them.

As to our "man about town," he managed very well to ward off all attempts to influence him. Though he had been for several months at our school, no transference was established in the psychoanalytic sense. One could notice nevertheless that the Ober-Hollabrunn surroundings had not been without effect even in his case. I wanted him to be away for a very short time, so that the unattractiveness of another setting might lead him to realize the pleasure values contained in the milieu of Ober-Hollabrunn, making him thus more open to therapeutic intervention. However, to achieve this result one could not just send him away forcibly; he had to go on his own accord, as a free agent. Of course he must not have the slightest inkling of our purpose. It seemed obvious that the only means of fulfilling precisely these conditions was to influence his mood as to the comparative merits of life in and out of school. In fact, a half-hour talk proved enough to bring back to his mind a strongly positive picture of the "outer" world; and barely an hour had elapsed before his counselor brought the news that he had run away. The first part of the "educational treatment" had succeeded; the pupil had been attracted outward, irresistibly. I should add that his counselor did not know that this escape had been provoked. (Whenever I make such an experiment, I inform the teacher only if the latter's cooperation is really indispensable, since it is very difficult for one who lives among the pupils to avoid giving himself away. And whether the experiment succeeds or remains fruitless, it makes occasion for endless discussions.) Concerning the second part of an educational treatment in this particular case—I mean the establishment of a transference—you shall hear later.

Another example is intervention in the acute conflicts connected with stealing. In one such case, instead of acting merely on intuition, I went so far as to create the needed situation deliberately. I had read Otto Rank's *The Incest Motive in Poetry and Saga* (1912). While thinking about the Aristotelian doctrine of catharsis, it occurred to me that we could perhaps use our own pupils' conflicts and make one of our boys the hero of a drama. Conflicts in thievery seemed appropriate. The opportunity for such an experiment soon arose.

We had an eighteen-year-old who had been expelled from a military school for stealing from his comrades, and had been guilty of thefts at home and elsewhere. As a part of my plan, after a few months with us, I put him in charge of the tobacco shop. (Our employees contributed each a certain amount of money to buy their tobacco in common.) The total weekly amount reached 700 to 800 Austrian crowns, which was a relatively large sum in those days. I asked our cashier to keep an unobtrusive eye on the young man and to report to me if and when any money was missing. After about four weeks, the report came in that 450 crowns had been pocketed. It seemed to me that I had now the proper occasion of exposing the pupil to shock and emotion so as to bring about catharsis, although I had no idea how to start. Wanting first of all to gain time, I told the cashier to send the youth to my office in the afternoon, without letting him know that the disappearance of the money had been noticed.

The boy came, but I was still in doubt about how to proceed. I wanted to keep him with me for a time and therefore suggested that he might help me in dusting my books and putting them in order.

I had to act in such a way that the boy himself would remain in the center of the action; the "drama" must develop so as to arouse his anxiety and to increase it to the point of unbearable intensity. At the moment when catastrophe would seem unavoidable to him, the crisis should be given such a turn that anxiety would change abruptly into emotional outburst. This sudden contrast in affects would cause an excitation which might bring about, or at least pave the way, for therapy.

In the present instance, the "dramatic play" develops as follows. We begin to dust the books. I ask him how he is getting along in school, and gradually approach the subject of the tobacco shop. "How much money do you take in per week?" "Between 700 and 800 crowns." We continue putting the books in order. After some time, I ask again: "Does your cash always come out right?" I hear a halting "Yes," of which I take no notice. Again after a pause: "When do you sell most of your tobacco?" "Before noon." Then a little later, I add: "Some day I must drop in and have a look at your cashbox." The boy grows visibly restive, yet I pretend to ignore it and to go on working with him, or rather upon him, coming back again and again to the matter of tobacco and cash. When his uneasiness reached the point which I deem proper for a climax, I put him suddenly before the dreaded decision: "Listen, when we are through with our work here, I will go and have a look at your cashbox." (We had been together for about an hour and a quarter.) He stands with his back to me, facing the bookshelves; he takes a book from a shelf to dust it but lets it fall to the ground. Now finally I take notice of his excitement. "What is the matter?" "Nothing. . . ." "You are short of cash? How much?" His face is disfigured by fear, he barely manages to stammer: "Four hundred and fifty crowns." Without a single word, I hand him over the precise amount. He glances at me with an indescribable expression and wants to speak out. But I do not let him talk, because I feel that my own action must exert its full effect upon him. I just send him away with a friendly nod and an encouraging gesture of the hand. After about ten minutes, he comes back, lays the 450 crowns on my desk, and adds: "Have me locked up, I don't deserve your help, I will certainly steal again. . . ." These words, spoken in a paroxysm of emotion, are drowned in bitter sobbing. I let him sit down and start a man-to-man talk with him. Of course I refrain from preaching morals to him, but listen sympathetically to all he pours out: his thieving, his attitude toward family and life, and everything else that burdens him. The initial, exceptionally strong affect subsides by and by, relieved by talking and weeping. Finally, I hand him the money once more, assuring him that I do not believe he would steal again, and that anyhow he is well worth 450 crowns to me. Furthermore, I add, this amount is not a gift; he could smoke less, save some money, and pay me back gradually. But so that nobody should notice that anything is amiss, he must put the 450 crowns back in the cashbox. Afterwards, I explained to our cashier that the sum had been restored and that he should ignore the matter as if he had never been aware of it. Actually, within the next two months, the boy paid all the money back to me.

It seems probable that the solution had resulted from the great difference in tension between the anxiety which gripped the boy when he perceived that I was aware of his stealing, and his relief at seeing the situation develop otherwise than he expected. From the practical, educational standpoint, the treatment had been successfully completed; indeed, afterwards, during the short time he stayed with us, the youth behaved quite decently. Since then he has been employed as a draftsman in a big furniture factory in Vienna, where he is doing very well.

Thus we had succeeded in arousing a strong emotion and in using it for educational purposes. Further experience is required with this method before we can judge whether it may yet develop into a special technique, and if so, in what cases it should be applied.

I once had occasion to remark, in this connection, that we should consider it a natural occurrence when inmates go on thieving in a reform school; indeed, in certain cases it seemed necessary to provide the pupil with opportunities for theft. I then heard from outside people that it was highly regrettable, even though perhaps understandable, if stealing did occur within an institution for the rehabilitation of delinquents; but that it was quite absurd to consider theft as a necessary phase of education.

Let us return, after this digression, to the description of the environment which I deem indispensable for the retraining of wayward youth.

The spirit which permeates the training school must proceed from the educators themselves, from their own positive attitude toward life; it must flow from a philosophy that irradiates cheerfulness and joy. Only thus will the counselors be able to approach their wards closely enough to attract them throughout the various phases of training and make them feel always that they are being understood. Among these juvenile delinquents, the need for tenderness which is inherent in childhood has very seldom been satisfied. Many of them have skipped an entire phase of development; the early years of their childhood have been followed by a ruthless struggle for life; they have never experienced that wonderful world of the fairy tales which often brightens even the later years of a man's lifetime; nor have they ever lived through the happy hours of intimate closeness between mother and child. To such young people, much should be given; and only a teacher who is himself a person of great intuitive delicacy may succeed in divining the right approach in every case. He cannot rely here on any science of pedagogy. If such capacity for intuition is a typically feminine quality, then we must give preference—in the retraining of delinquents—to educators who possess feminine traits of character. More than that: we cannot dispense with women in the re-education of male youth. The asocial child, or young man, hides much of his own inner experiences, either consciously or as a result of unconscious reasons. Without a refined intuition, we risk missing the mark in our educational endeavors. It is not enough to grasp the meaning of what a pupil says and does; the real educator must be able so to identify himself with his ward that the latter's experiences become like his own.

If delinquency is to be cured and the asocial youth made fit again for life in society, the training school must provide him with new ties and induce him to attach himself to persons of his environment. We try to bring about such attachments by the kindly manner in which we treat our pupils. Naturally, despite all our good intentions, the reform school is no paradise and we cannot always avoid having conflicts and negative moods. Almost from the beginning of our work in Ober-Hollabrunn I observed especially in those groups led by women counselors that if the woman happened to be in a bad mood, this mood would spread immediately to the entire group; conversely, the collective antagonism which had been created in that way would react upon the teacher herself; and this reciprocal action would increase until it broke out in open conflicts. I called this phenomenon "the downward influence." It manifested itself also when the director happened to be in a bad mood which would gradually reach the entire organization.

At that time I did not yet understand the releasing effect produced by talking things over. However, I noticed again and again how completely the situation in a group reversed itself when we succeeded in lifting the spirits of its woman counselor. Through repeated personal talks with each individual teacher on our staff, in which we often dealt with confidential matters, I succeeded gradually in establishing a relationship of mutual trust with my collaborators. The reciprocal quality of this relationship spread in turn to our pupils, so that the same feeling tone dominated the whole institution. None of our authority was sacrificed in the process. In this way we replaced any fears which our wards might have harbored against us by feelings of well-earned confidence.

Later on, the mechanism of transference as disclosed by the teachings of psychoanalysis provided us with a rational explanation of our educational success. It showed me also why it is so easy to talk about pedagogic problems, while the practical ability to bring up children can be acquired only through experience. What succeeds with one teacher may fail entirely with another who imitates him. I consider it impossible for the staff of a training school to work successfully without a strong attachment to the school's director. I cannot conceive that a delinquent child can be re-educated as a social being without attachment to a person of his own environment; the counselor's attitude toward his own leader will also determine for the most part the attitude of the pupil toward his counselor.

In a retraining institution, it is obviously impractical to assign a counselor to each single pupil. The numerical size of a group is determined by the available financial means as well as by pedagogic considerations. Educators will always insist on having the smallest possible units. At present, our groups consist of twenty-five pupils. Each group has its own playroom, dormitory, and separate washroom, and forms an autonomous cell within the structure of the school.

In reformatories of the old type, each group is an indiscriminate collection of unrelated cases, which can only aggravate the pathological conditions of individual children. It is evident that one cannot re-educate such a heterogeneous crowd, one can only try to keep it within bounds by compulsory means. This may be one of the reasons why it never seems possible to dispense with corporal punishment in correctional institutions of the old type.

When Dr. Lazar came to Ober-Hollabrunn, he undertook the experiment of forming groups according to this diagnostic viewpoint. As he explains (Lazar, 1920), he had to abandon this project as quite impractical, because the several psychopathological forms which had been established diagnostically were not homogeneous enough for the needs of pedagogy. Because of that, he set himself the task of working out a method of grouping which would first of all take into account the various temperaments of the counselors and the requirements of educational leadership.

At Ober-Hollabrunn, Lazar found a soil which had already been broken for his investigation. At first, the inmates had been segregated only according to sex and to age, school children and older groups; otherwise, they had been kept together in heterogeneous groups, in the order in which they had come to us. But this method had soon resulted in extraordinary difficulties of leadership. Individual pupils had to be removed from their group and shifted about among other units until they could be handled without excessive disturbance. Thus our earliest system of grouping arose simply from the practical needs of educational leadership.

In the several groups there remained finally only those pupils who banded together of their own accord. One teacher, Martin Krämer, a man gifted with extraordinary insight for distinguishing the various juvenile characters, was able to pick out the mutually suitable candidates from the chaotic crowd, quite independently of any theory of group formation. He could easily determine what was the right group for each newcomer. It was therefore no longer necessary to let the new pupil wander tentatively from one group to another.

From Lazar's studies it appeared that our group had become an organic entity. Taking into account the intellectually
defective, the boys are grouped in the following categories,
as described by Lazar (1920):

I.   Intellectual defects;
II.  Social deficiencies which can be remedied without
     particular difficulties through the influence of the new
     environment;
III. Social deficiencies which have deeper and stronger
     roots and require, in addition to the influence of the
     new environment, active retraining;
IV.  Characterological failures in addition to social defi-
     ciencies, but with a relatively high intelligence;
V.   Disturbances in the mental equilibrium, with moti-
     vated aggressiveness, in addition to characterological
     failures and social deficiencies;
VI.  Aggressiveness of various kinds, breaking out without
     motivation.

We now had groups which comprised similar elements;
their typical characteristics would be easily grasped by each
counselor, who could not fail to sense them through the
mere repetition within the group. The counselor was therefore enabled to adjust himself to such types. Furthermore, he
could now apply to good effect a fairly uniform method of
education, because he need no longer struggle with sharply
contrasted characters within the same group. As to the pupils
themselves, the way in which they had been brought together
provided them with conditions favorable for their development and rehabilitation. This principle of grouping proved
to be at once economical and justified from the standpoint
of educational therapy.

After we had completed our first group adjustments in
Ober-Hollabrunn, there still remained twelve boys of school
age who, because of their exceptional aggressiveness, could
not be admitted in any of the existing units and whom we
therefore had to put into a separate group. I stress again

that these boys were by far our most troublesome cases. Extremely violent outbreaks of rage often occurred without any adequate motivation. Fights arose repeatedly, in which the boys assaulted each other with table knives, hurled dishes at each other, overturned the stove, used a firebrand as a weapon, etc. We had to find a proper approach. The majority of our staff were of the opinion that we needed a somewhat stiffer discipline coupled with much physical activity; but I myself was inclined to take the opposite view: we should first of all try to discover the causes of their aggressiveness. If I remember rightly, my proposal was backed only by our consultant psychologist. I therefore decided to take upon myself the leadership of this group, with the help of two women counselors who had volunteered for the difficult task.

I am reporting about this "aggressive" group, because our educational endeavors brought us new insight into the treatment of juvenile delinquents.

To start with, I did not concern myself overmuch with the case history of each boy, as it had been pieced together by social workers from the youth welfare agency and forwarded to us with the other official papers at the time of the pupil's admission to our school. I wanted to learn from the child himself what was his attitude toward life and how his experiences were reflected in his behavior. Repeated and exhaustive interviews with each boy showed the following: in every case there was a severe conflict between the two parents, or between the child and his parents. The children had acquired a hate relationship in respect to father or mother, or both of them, or in respect to their stepparents or foster parents. None of the children had had his natural needs for affection satisfied. In some instances, the normal feelings of love had been entirely transferred from the human being to an animal. Of their pet rabbits they would speak with the greatest tenderness, but in the very next moment they would threaten their fellow pupils with bodily violence. All the boys had suffered unmerciful beatings and so they were prone to hit back, or even to attack without provocation, whenever they felt themselves to be the strongest.

Once these facts had been elucidated, there was for me no doubt whatsoever about the course we should pursue. Our treatment was to be: absolute mildness and friendliness; continual occupation and much play, so as to forestall outbreaks of aggressiveness; repeated personal interviews with each pupil.

Our gentleness was often construed as weakness. Their reaction, pushed to a ridiculous point of exaggeration, was that we were the ones who were afraid! The acts of aggression, therefore, became more intense and more frequent. In addition to assaulting each other in an increasingly violent manner, they started destroying the furniture in their own bungalow. Windowpanes were broken, door panels kicked in. One boy jumped through a closed double window, caring little about the injuries he might suffer from the splintered glass. Finally, the dinner table was deserted, because each boy sought for himself a corner in the playroom where he would crouch on the floor to devour his meal. Screaming and howling could be heard from afar; the bungalow looked really like an insane asylum.

The two women teachers assigned to the group were in a state nearing despair, for I continued to insist that the boys be allowed to work off their aggressiveness, and that the counselors should not intervene except when necessary to prevent injury. Absolute impartiality was required in the fights and quarrels; the boys should be kept busy as much as possible, with play and other activities to divert them from mischief; the teachers must be equally nice to all and maintain their composure at all costs; in brief, they had to perform the function of a center of peace in the middle of chaos. The two educators (Ida Leibfried and Grete Schmid) strove to accomplish this task with extraordinary devotion, but they were finally so exhausted as to need replacement. Two other women counselors (Gerta Grabner and Valerie Kremer) volunteered and worked, if possible, with an even greater en-

thusiasm and spirit of sacrifice. In fact, we owe the solution
of the problem chiefly to their courageous perseverance.

In spite of all the difficulties, I still persisted in following
the prescribed path, because I perceived the effects of our
treatment on the behavior of the boys. Instead of genuine
acts of aggression we could now observe instances of pseudo
aggressiveness. The most indescribable excesses on the part
of the inmates failed to arouse our opposition. In the children's former environment, much less objectionable conduct
sufficed to bring about a reaction of brutality on the
part of their elders. Our own attitude, which was incomprehensible to the boys, induced them to commit further and
more savage misdeeds, which, however, could not increase
beyond a certain point of climax. But the response, definitely
awaited according to the child's earlier experience—a slap in
the face, perhaps, or a kick in the back—still failed to occur.
Yet to them it simply *had* to come, for otherwise the hate
impulse would have lacked any further justification. Therefore, after a period of increasing aggressions, we could observe the phenomenon of pseudo aggressiveness. But as the
latter also failed to elicit from us that reaction which was
unconsciously desired by the boys, its place was now taken
by another affect, tears of rage. I remember an incident
which seemed particularly revolting. In my presence, one of
our pupils, swinging a bread knife, hurled himself upon another boy, put the knife at his throat and yelled: "You dirty
dog, I'll stab you to death!" I stood by unruffled, doing nothing to protect the victim, and taking no notice of the
imminent danger which seemed to threaten him. For it was
clear to me that this was a typical case of pseudo aggression.
In fact, seeing that I refused to become alarmed, the pretended cutthroat promptly threw his knife to the floor, flew
into a rage, stamped his feet, and after some inarticulate
howls broke down completely, weeping violently, until he
was so exhausted that he finally fell alseep.

After such hysterical outbursts there usually followed a
period of great emotional instability. For a time the children

would behave well, or at least tolerably well, with no aggressiveness whatsoever; but later the outbreaks of rage
would be worse than before.

My conviction was, and still is, that the remedial treatment of delinquency is brought about through unconscious
processes; and that it is often carried to a successful end by
an unexpected climax, or "miracle"—in the sense illustrated,
for instance, by the story of the 450 crowns stolen in the
tobacco shop. I therefore perceived in the case of our "aggressive" group that the time was ripe for letting the boys
experience a strong affect of joy—because, indeed, the periods
of good behavior were now lasting longer and longer. The
Christmas holidays were approaching. I thought that the fes-
tival, with its traditional gifts, would provide a proper occasion for completing the catharsis. The holiday was cele-
brated joyfully, with deep inner effectiveness. The crisis was
over. A great change had certainly taken place when, only a
few days later, we abandoned our devastated bungalow, the
witness of so many ugly scenes, and moved into new quarters,
completely renovated, which promised a better life. Some
people had advised us against doing so, for they could not
conceive why the most reckless crew in all our establishment
should be lodged in the nicest of our bungalows.

It is true that the children remained for a while in a state
of sensitivity. Our consultant psychologist, Franz Winkel-
mayer, entrusted with the task of educating them, showed
great ability in leading this difficult group. Gradually and
very cautiously, he increased the demands made on the pupils.
Quite intentionally, he was not always even-tempered and
friendly; in fact, he showed impatience, dissatisfaction, bad
moods, etc.—in short, all the reactions which the boys would
encounter in normal life. I need hardly add that these formerly aggressive inmates now became particularly devoted
students.

It is a point of interest that several of these pupils, in the
period after their aggressiveness had subsided, showed superior intellectual performance. The libidinal problem here
involved certainly deserves further study.

We have tried to explain to ourselves the nature of this curative process. I sum up the facts: while we let the other groups form themselves simply by leaving together those pupils who got along with each other, we had no choice but to keep the twelve aggressive boys as a separate group. It was only to be expected—and this was also the opinion of our staff—that this artificial, unwieldy crowd of juvenile delinquents would have to be handled by coercive means. But we experienced quite the contrary. The fact is that our "aggressive" group proved to be a coherent unit, in which the pupils were able to recover their capacity for social life, although we excluded every means of coercion.

In agreement with Freud's conclusions in *Group Psychology and the Analysis of the Ego* (1921), we conceive of this process in the following way: after a period of increasing aggressiveness, the boys developed a strong emotional attachment to the women counselors, to myself, and later to our psychologist. This intensive object attachment resulted in due course in a mutual identification of all the pupils, and therefore in a mutual emotional relationship. This kept the group together. No other force could possibly account for such a result. As we have stressed already, no external pressure was applied to prevent the group from falling apart.

In cases of aggressiveness, the libido, whatever its source, is used up in similar manifestations of asocial behavior. It is worth while to examine how this libido expresses itself after a successful cure.

We have already seen that in spite of every act of savagery our counselors were not to be bullied into an attitude of opposition. The pupils responded at first with a feeling of possessing more power than their teachers, which again led to more frequent and violent explosions of aggressiveness; then the reaction gave way to tears of rage, followed by a period of great emotional instability, and finally by good behavior.

The discharge of affect through tears of rage was, technically speaking, an "abreaction." It effected the loosening of the previously stable structure of aggressiveness, and lessened the sadomasochistic impulses against the woman teacher.

After each of these discharges, the normal, tender libido, which had previously been repressed, found less and less opposition and was gradually enabled to assert itself, taking hold of an appropriate object, in this case the woman teacher (cathexis). Once the transference had been established, there developed by and by an emotional attachment (identification) to the fellow inmates, who were themselves involved in the same process of educational taming. We could observe the remarkable phenomenon of how the isolated, individual delinquents began to integrate themselves emotionally in a social group or "mass." The loosening up of the asocial behavior, progressing more and more explosively, liberates more and more of that libido which had formerly served to sustain delinquency, and which is now free for normal reaction. Still, we do not know whether a sufficient amount of this previously obnoxious libido has been sublimated, so as to exclude the possibility of the child's reverting to the old asocial ways, in the event of return to his earlier environment with its selfsame conflicts. After all, our duty is not only to cure him, but to make him *immune,* before sending him back to the "infected" area. Consequently, we should expose him to various influences while he is still in the training school. This could be accomplished only by making him join, for shorter or longer periods, the various other groups in the institution. This cannot be done, unfortunately, because it would mean that a number of pupils would wander all the time from group to group, and none of the units would be left in peace to perform its specific educational task. Nevertheless, we found some sort of solution by creating a special "In and Out" group.

In that way, we solved the problem of how to treat the most difficult cases in a reform institution. Anybody wanting to check on the validity of our method should not overlook, however, that he must also create the same conditions in which we carried out our own experiment.

The question may be asked whether similar or perhaps much better results could not be obtained by other means. If

we were to psychoanalyze a considerable numb
which appeared similar to us, we might be able
gether, with increasing exactitude, those who
comparable; we would thus have gained an unobjec-
basis for experimenting with more selective groups. We
would also learn whether a grouping of comparable cases
really offers the best conditions for remedial treatment of
juvenile delinquency; we would discover what are the complexes that produce similar manifestations in antisocial behavior; and what are the cases that cannot be treated within
a single group, etc. Only then would our methods of grouping
be based upon sufficient psychological insight, and only then
would the entire theory of group formation be capable of
further development.

The juvenile delinquents whose plight induced us to approach them with mildness, kindness, and friendliness are
the same who, in reformatories of the old type, compel the
staff to take an attitude of stern opposition; life in such
institutions is therefore toned down (or if you wish, toned
up) to the well-known level of sadomasochism. Our method
has now become public property, and so far we have not
found it necessary to modify our approach. We are still the
friend and adviser of those children and youths who become our wards, we try to satisfy their needs and to show
understanding for their weaknesses. If objection is raised that
our attitude does not fit the case of all pupils in reform
institutions, then the answer is simply that we have not yet
gained sufficient experience. We shall change methods only
when we are compelled to do so by our own increased
knowledge.

We do not try to influence the newly admitted pupil by
soft words; we put him instead in the so-called "In and Out"
group. We do not attempt to win him over at that stage; we
just wait until a transference is achieved, although we do of
course try to speed up the process whenever it seems overdue.

In the case of our seventeen-year-old gambler and "man
about town" (see above), we had successfully provoked this

pupil into running away, which was only the first act in a drama calculated to achieve a transference. Indeed, I expected the boy to return on the second day. When he had not come back after a full week, I began to wonder whether my intervention had not been an utter mistake.

On the tenth day, at half past nine in the evening, someone knocked at the door of my apartment. Franz was back. He was exhausted physically, and in such a state of psychological tension that I felt able at once to accomplish much more with him than I had intended at the time when I planned this pedagogic "provocation." I did not reproach him in any manner for his desertion, although he evidently expected the most bitter reproaches; I only looked at him seriously for a short while, and then asked him without further transition: "When did you last eat?" "Yesterday evening." I took him into our dining room and made him sit at the table where the family was having supper. Franz, who was prepared for anything except such a reception, lost his composure entirely and was so upset that he could not eat at all. Although I aware of this, I asked him: "Why aren't you eating?" "I can't. May I eat outside the dining room?" "Yes, go to the kitchen." His plate was refilled several times, until he was no longer hungry. It was ten o'clock by then. I went to the kitchen and said to him: "It is now very late, you cannot return to your group tonight. You will sleep in my apartment." I fixed a couch for him in the anteroom, and Franz went to bed; I patted him on the head and wished him good night. The very next morning the transference was in full effect, so that from then on his re-education went forward very fast. What a strongly positive transference it was I learned from a mistake which I made sometime later. I gave him grounds for jealousy, quite unintentionally of course: I showed preference to one of his comrades in some office work. My incautiousness was brought back to me when Franz committed an act of revenge which was psychoogically quite enlightening. Fortunately, I succeeded in repairing the error. Today Franz is a well-trained businessman and an assistant clerk in our own office; he drives a truck and supplies us with foodstuffs and other commodities from Vienna; merchandise worth millions of Austrian crowns is entrusted to him.

This case is naturally an exception: only very rarely does one need such artful devices in order to establish a transference. As a rule, it is enough to treat a pupil with gentle equanimity, while showing alternately disregard and appreciation for his conduct.

The curative education of the individual begins only after a transference has been established. We do not educate with words, speeches, or admonitions, with bad marks or punishments, but we lead the pupils through those vital experiences that result in their social reintegration. Where this method of leadership is rightly applied, every child will be made to experience for himself the daily adventure of living; and whether such experiences seem insignificant or important to the outsider, they will deeply affect the pupil himself. One can always bring about the various situations that may create precisely the desired moods. The romanticism of the gangster, the ideal of a modern Robin Hood, so strongly emphasized in every asocial child, offers many opportunities in this respect.

We have no universal prescription for the training school educator. Every teacher must try to find the right way according to his own personality. He can learn much through careful observation, painstaking work, and earnest study— provided he possesses the ability of being a teacher. But the dilettante, as well as the professional social worker who has no real calling for his profession, can do nothing but harm in the education of wayward youth.

Our conception of how to handle the pupils may perhaps seem something to be taken for granted. But I deem it only fair to mention that our methods often make tremendous demands upon ourselves. Let us not forget the wide gap between recognizing the rightness of a procedure and basing one's own conduct in life upon such recognition.

To explain what are the particular means we use in our pedagogy, I am rather at a loss for a reply. For we have no prescribed rules. For punishment, we simply withhold or withdraw any rewards we might have given. If acts of rudeness are committed, or if thefts occur, I have the culprit sent to me for a man-to-man talk. Such interviews, and a gentle attitude of forgiveness, have always proved to be the best educational method.

If talking things over serves us well, it is only because we have gained the confidence of our pupils. They come to us with all the difficulties which they cannot overcome by themselves; with all their uncertainties and complaints, their hopes and aspirations, and a thousand questions which they ask themselves about the unknown. But they also come with their own ideas and convictions, often acquired through painful struggles. Many innermost doubts swim up to the surface; torturing misconceptions about religious truths; stifling oppression of the inconceivable; rejection of all church practices; scorn for any feeling of faith, even one's own, to the point of hate against every religion; but at times also quite genuine and deeply religious experiences. We must proceed here with great caution, explaining and instructing, sometimes clearing away many misunderstandings and erroneous notions—but always careful to avoid the danger of forcing our own convictions upon the pupils.

At other times, they come in embarrassment, with flushed cheeks and unsteady glances, to tell haltingly about their first infatuations, their most delicate love dreams, their amorous imaginations, and also to share with us everything that is beautiful, or unbearable, in the experience of real love. They show themselves in the role of Don Juan or of Sir Galahad; they come to us with their sexual troubles, their suffering, their vices. It is only seldom—in special cases which seem to require it—that we ourselves lead the talk to sex topics. Perhaps it would interest you to learn that in our washrooms there are none of those obscene drawings and scribblings which are usually found in such places.

Such interviews might also result in a proper grouping of the pupils; indeed, their behavior during these talks, however much it may seem to vary from one case to another, reveals nevertheless a number of common tendencies.

The intellectually deficient show up immediately. Beside the variations in intelligence, one is struck by other glaring differences. Individual attitudes toward the environment can also offer a means of classification. Two types of hate reaction are easily distinguished. The one type faces the environment with feelings of hatred, which may not always be strongly expressed, but are nonetheless easy to perceive in the form of a definite hostility. If one studies the individual cases by placing them in a series of increasingly hostile manifestations, from silent repudiation to deadly hatred, then it is easy to notice their common denominator, their inner relationship to the world.

The second type of hate is not so widespread. I found it most often among girls, and for some inconceivable reason among the boys who happened to be of Jewish descent. Such pupils are obliging to the degree of obnoxiousness, friendly to the point of unpleasant intimacy, self-conscious to the verge of arrogance; they are also cunning liars and intriguers; they reveal themselves by becoming the tyrants of their fellow inmates and the secret instigators of trouble. All these manifestations should be interpreted as reactions of hatred.

I have always found that hate is a reaction to an unsatisfied need for love. This is something which in many cases could be established objectively; though in still more cases it arises merely from the child's subjective feeling. In the first type, we are probably dealing with the results of insufficient love bestowed upon the child, or of a brutal repudiation of the child by his elders. As to the second type, here we are perhaps confronted with the paradox of too much love, mostly lavished by the mother.

In the latter cases—as we were able to ascertain from talks with the parents—there had always been too little love between husband and wife, and therefore the mother had taken refuge in her feelings toward the child. But the child, in his turn, must have felt cheated, for he could perceive that this love was not given to him for his own sake; and his reaction would manifest itself in delinquent behavior.

In each of these two types of juvenile delinquency the hate reaction is expressed in a quite characteristic manner: open rebellion to the point of brutal murder, or, on the contary, underhandedness ending in times in the cowardly assassination of a victim asleep.

The following letter shows how a pupil belonging to the second type attempts to discredit the training school through his own feelings of hatred.

St. Andrä, May 3, 1922

Dear Parents:

It is generally believed here that I will stay in this place only until the end of the proceedings;[4] also, that they cannot have me jailed, because I belong to an educational institution. After the proceedings are over, in a favorable way, you will take me back home: so I was told by the Director.[5] He did not make a secret of it; all the pupils know it already. Then he also said: "I have no objection if your mother takes you home; for you are giving me more trouble than our whole establishment. I shall recite the *Pater Noster* prayer if ever I succeed in finding some job for you in town. You can really believe me when I say so," he added.

Mr. Krämer says just the same thing as the Director. I have swallowed two bottles of ink[6] and when Mr. Krämer learned about it he said that if I ever swallow more ink, I shall have to pay 200 crowns for each bottle. I owe it to Mr. Müller [the counselor of his group] if I am

[4] His trial in the appellate court, for large-scale thefts of merchandise and stealings in private homes.

[5] This and the following statements are strongly exaggerated, or for the most part freely invented.

[6] He had asked both teachers and pupils whether it was very dangerous to swallow ink, and how it tasted; he received the answer that only a large amount could be harmful. Shortly afterwards, in the presence of the office workers, he took a sip from an inkstand and spat out the ink immediately.

still alive; in fact, I was leaning outside the window[7] when he happened to come by, and he got hold of me and dragged me back. The Director then said that he would not keep me any more; he did not want to bring discredit[8] to an institution of which he has been the leader for such a long time, and which had the reputation of being the very best. Therefore, I beg you, come and take me, one of you. The Director said also that he would write a letter, either to the Tribunal for Juvenile Delinquents, or to you. Bring me some soap, right away, for here we have only such kind as gives no lather,[9] though all the group has to wash with it. Bring also a pair of shoes, if possible, for I am already wearing the red ones every day, because that boy took away my slippers again; we are not allowed to go barefoot here, and my feet hurt terribly in these shoes. Mr. Krämer said, furthermore, that all this is bunk, I am on slippery ground and will get at least three months. He is a very unreliable fellow, but still he added that he is curious to know how the next proceedings develop. There is one more thing I want to mention about this ink I swallowed: I only got headaches and fits of dizziness, otherwise there was nothing wrong with me. Nevertheless, they keep an eye on me to prevent further mischief. Mr. Müller has discussed my case with the Director, from 9 to 11 P.M., and I am now being watched as if I were a convict. The teacher who is on night duty keeps most of the time near my bed and checks every now and then whether I am already asleep.[10] That is the way I am being treated since yesterday.

Give my best regards to everybody.

Your son, who begs for your forgiveness,

Siegfried

Another letter:

You will see how everything will be better when I get a

[7] He was eating, as pupils often do, on the inner side of the window sill—which was more than three feet wide—when Mr. Müller passed by.

[8] I told him to his face that all he wanted to achieve was to bring our training school into ill repute. (The letter was not the only such attempt.)

[9] Pupils receive ordinary soap which gives plenty of lather; what the boy wanted was fancy toilet soap.

[10] Completely untrue.

job, as soon as possible. For, next year in February, I will already be a *Kannui*.[11] I shall not steal any more, God forbid. Dear parents, I see it all now, what shame I brought upon you. But I will improve my ways from now on. I assure you, next year you shall say: "Such a son as ours is not easy to be found." When I get myself a job, I will work with all my heart and patience, so as to please my boss. I will then become a *Kannui* in February 1923, and remain at my job so as to earn a one-year certificate. Those who have such a certificate are given preference everywhere. You cannot imagine how sorry I am for you; I am actually weeping while I write this letter, you may believe me. I am crying each time I think of you. I can see now how very dumb I was. I beg for your forgiveness with both my hands raised; please do forgive a son who now recognizes his errors. Dear Daddy, please come to visit me on Sunday, don't refuse this one request, otherwise I don't know what I shall do to myself. I can imagine how many sacrifices I have cost you, but everything will be repaid to you, in your old age, with interest and even with compound interest. Think only that whatever I may have cost you since my childhood is like a capital which will begin to bear interest in a few years. Someday you shall be glad that I am your son.

Your deeply repentant son,<br>Siegfried

The immediate reason which prompted Siegfried to write this letter was his ill-humor. Teacher Krämer, who had accompanied him to the appellate court for juvenile delinquents in Vienna, did not allow Siegfried to stay for several days in the city, as the boy wished; and the complaint which was lodged with me concerning this matter failed to have the expected success. In the present instance, it proved impossible to persuade Siegfried's mother that the letter which she had received from her son was full of inaccuracies and outright lies, although the youth had written the very same day to his grandmother also, and described himself as entirely satisfied.

---

[11] Untranslatable idiomatic expression, indicating an advance in status.

In such cases, which are by no means exceptional, it is difficult, sometimes quite impossible, to furnish proof. Mothers hover with exaggerated tenderness over children of this kind. They are always worrying, and are prone to believe that their darling does not receive sufficient attention. They are not aware, and do not let themselves be persuaded, that the pupil exploits this motherly solicitude for his conscious or unconscious attacks against his teachers. "The child's assertions could not have come out of thin air," such is the usual belief held by these kind souls. The youth has thus attained the goal at which he aimed from the beginning, namely, to harm the reputation of the training school. He celebrates his greatest triumph when the misguided mother finally shows up to take her son home. That he will shortly reappear at the reform institution, simply because he cannot be managed at home, is something which neither son nor mother suspect at the moment.[12]

It now remains for me to touch upon the subject of our "abnormal" charges, the depressives, the hypersensitives, the depressive-hypersensitives, and those who have suffered one single severe psychic trauma. In their behavior during interviews they differ completely from the types described above. To us they were quite isolated cases, until we read Freud's studies of "Mourning and Melancholia" (1917). Sinch then we can see that they belong in a definite category, which may offer some prospects of pedagogic investigation and treatment. We even feel that we have discovered a point of attack, which should enable us, starting from the phenomenon of narcissism, to put the retraining of delinquents in a new light.

Before ending this lecture, I wish to define my position in regard to psychoanalysis.

I owe it to the science of psychoanalysis if I now understand my own attitude, formerly quite intuitive, toward the

---

[12] Siegfried was taken away from the training school, shortly after writing this letter. But at present he finds himself again in a reformatory, at Eggenburg, for having embezzled once more a considerable sum of money.

educational staff and toward the pupils; and this new understanding has allowed me to straighten out many things and
to strive for further improvement.

Psychoanalysis has brought to me an understanding of
complexes that are effective unconsciously, and a comprehension of trauma which often determines delinquency.

It has taught me to use for educational purposes the mechanisms of transference, sublimation, and compensation.

At present, psychoanalysis appears to me as the only psychological method which permits one to grasp the mental
condition of a pupil at the time he is being subjected to
pedagogical handling.

We educators expect that psychoanalysis should help us in
the future to cure individual cases directly, and that it should
give us the means of discovering the unconscious causes of
asocial behavior, in order to work out effective and economical methods for the remedial treatment of delinquency.

We demand that every educator be himself psychoanalyzed,
so that he may correct any distortions within himself. Otherwise such deformations would distort his personal and professional attitude toward life. Consequently, we demand that
the psychoanalyst should find his place in the framework of
the training school for wayward youth.

On the other hand, we deem it inadvisable, for reasons of
transference, that the pupil should be analyzed by his own
teacher.

# II

# On the Problem of Wayward Youth

In both higher and elementary schools there are pupils who compel the teacher to distract his attention from his proper duties as a pedagogue and prevent the entire class from reaching the prescribed goals in study and education. Among such children and juveniles, the "delinquents" form a group of a particular kind. Although they differ widely from each other in their attitudes and although their various forms of behavior are highly differentiated, manifestations of delinquency seem nevertheless so characteristic that this type is well known to every teacher. For a discussion of delinquency, further definition of waywardness is unnecessary.

Since both teacher and pupils are expected to work according to certain curricular standards, every delinquent child endangers the timely fulfillment of this task. In proportion to the number of wayward children in a classroom, and depending upon the sharpness of their individual manifestations of waywardness, lessons in the class will be disrupted and the teacher will have to take a definite stand. But the reaction of the teacher himself will depend upon his own

---

"Zum Verwahrlosten Problem." *Zeitschrift für psychoanalytische Pädagogik,* 1:25-27, 1926-27.
Introduction to a series of essays.

attitude toward the delinquent. If we gain some degree of insight into the origin of his attitude, we shall understand a great deal regarding juvenile delinquency and criminality in schools and in the public at large.

We shall not deal here with those conditions that may be described as states of psychic or moral, intellectual or physical delinquency; indeed, for the time being, we are interested not in the problem of waywardness, but in the person of the wayward juvenile; or, even more restrictively, we are interested only in that aspect of the delinquent pupil which affects the attitude of the teacher. It is his reaction to the acts of commission or omission by the asocial child (or whatever other name one gives to such children) that determines his own attitude to the child. We must learn to know the conditions in which such reactions originate.

In every collectivity, including that collectivity which we call a school, there exist certain rules which regulate collective life—whether such rules have developed spontaneously or have been imposed from above. Anyone whose conduct does not conform to these rules necessarily becomes conspicuous; the delinquent will stand out in a particular manner. He transgresses the prevailing norms with the conscious or unconscious intention of making himself conspicuous, of being unpleasant to other people, of harming them, of disrupting the community, of threatening its continued existence. The delinquent interferes with the work in the classroom, he interrupts the lessons, he loosens or undermines the discipline, etc. He appears to others as a disagreeable fellow, and the teacher develops a tendency to react defensively. The reason a delinquent pupil acts in this way is self-evident only in the most exceptional cases; therefore, the attitude of the teacher toward the delinquent is very seldom determined by rational knowledge; on the contrary, it springs originally from an affective, emotional reaction. If, in each case, the teacher were able to observe his own behavior exactly and to submit to self-criticism, he would soon discover that an emotional reaction had set in well before any rational check, and that the check had not always sufficed to produce an objective attitude. If such self-criticism is sufficiently searching, the observer will also notice that it is not the type and seriousness of the offense itself which determine the way a delinquent pupil should be judged; our attitude toward the delinquent depends not on the gravity of the misdemeanor as such but on the effect which the transgression may have upon ourselves. However, this effect does not pertain to the delinquent alone. It is determined also by the momentary psychological conditions in which we happen to find ourselves, as well as by our libidinal relations to the wayward child and to the rule which he has transgressed. The stronger our libidinal ties with the delinquent, and the weaker our emotional involvement in the broken law, the less are we affected by the disturbance, and the more innocuous the offense appears in our eyes. Our defensive measures will consequently be minor. This is true in the family, in the classroom, in the group in educational or reform institutions. It is true also in human society at large, though it may be less apparent there. Indeed, it is hardly visible at all in the framework of penal legislation and penal practice. And yet it exists even here, as one may see from a very elementary example: He who embezzles 50 shillings will be punished—other conditions being the same —much less severely than he who steals 500 shillings. Why? The thing may appear self-evident; and yet from the standpoint of society, it is logical only on the assumption that society takes up the defense of the person who has incurred the loss, and acts according to the tenet: an eye for an eye, a tooth for a tooth. In behaving in such a way, society is actually lagging behind the times, and responding to an emotional reaction which developed long ago in the history of mankind. Concerning the delinquent himself, we are not much enlightened either by the 50 shilling theft or by the stealing of the 500 shillings: both tell us only that there is something wrong with him. The thefts are symptoms indicating that there is some disturbance in the psychic mechanism from the point of view of social order. But neither the kind nor the magnitude of the disturbance, nor the possible remedy, can be learned from the amount of the money stolen.

Human nature being what it is, people are inclined to avoid unpleasantness and to try to remove or to render harmless anything that disturbs them; therefore it is understandable in a teacher that he would wish to put delinquent pupils out of his school—just as society acts toward anyone who does not fit into the social order and imperils it. Measures prescribed against the delinquent by our penal laws, and carried out in our penal practice, aim to fight rather than to eliminate that which is conceived as an evil. But society itself has been perceiving for a long time that its own behavior toward delinquent and criminal youths is not the right one; and better ways to solve the problem are being sought. Unfortunately, society does not know what is wrong, and applies its efforts not at the right point. The tendency is to raise the age limit for penal responsibility, to find new grounds for admitting extenuating circumstances. Probation and conditional sentencing have been introduced. This does not take into account those conditions which give a true understanding of the nature of waywardness. What has been achieved is merely a milder form of the old conception. Measures continue to be taken along the same lines as before. One acts not so much according to a new and deeper insight, but according to a different libidinal relationship with the delinquent and with the law. The wayward child has moved closer to us, while we have withdrawn from the law some of the libido which had been bestowed upon it in former days: this is why our emotional reaction in cases of transgression is not so violent as before, and the defensive measures not so severe. On the other hand, there are a great many persons motivated not by a better knowledge but by reaction formations originating in childhood, who see this greater leniency as a terrible danger for the future of mankind, and who assert that penal law has no other task than to fight delinquency, while the removal of the causes of delinquency belongs in the province of education [*Erziehung*]. These views might be acceptable if juveniles were no longer punishable according to penal law, and if the sphere of education were to be substantially increased. But then we would need a completely new outlook on education, especially in welfare education.

Attitudes which are the result of a person's own experience in life are not easily accessible to intellectual examination, as one sees in the ceaseless conflicts of opinions as to whether the inmates in reform schools should be treated severely and castigated, and corporal punishment re-established, or whether, on the contrary, they should be handled with mildness and kindness. The facts to be adduced in the forthcoming articles of the present series will show us that such discussions do not bring us any closer to a solution of the problem of welfare education.

As to ourselves, the welfare educators, we consider the delinquent juvenile as a sick patient to be treated. A physician who would treat his patient according to the effect which the latter's illness might have on his environment would make us smile. Yet this is exactly how people act when they concern themselves overmuch with the effects of wayward actions upon those persons whose very function is to bear patiently such behavior. One does succeed, perhaps, from time to time, in keeping oneself aloof from any emotional attitude toward the delinquent; nevertheless, the measures prescribed take into consideration chiefly those effects which the child's waywardness has on other persons. We question the parents, interrogate the relatives, inquire at the school, and go to the neighbors; we make a thorough investigation, and yet, somehow, we overlook the fact that all the data we have gathered so patiently concern not the wayward child himself but only the manner in which he is affecting his environment.

The welfare educator, the child guidance worker, has to ask himself the following questions: What attitude should I take? And how should I act? An answer can be found, even though we are still very far from knowing all there is to know. In some important respects, we are beginning to see the light, because we can now avail ourselves of the assistance of psychoanalysis, which gives us information about the child and about the conditions of his normal and abnormal development. It reveals the causes, and teaches us how to remove inhibitions and repair damages. For the welfare educator, this method is not only a psychological theory; it is also a means of learning more about himself and of bringing order into his own psychic household, so that he can create within himself those attitudes without which no educational welfare work could possibly be fruitful.

# III

# The Juvenile Court: Is It a Solution?

The two concepts "educational welfare work" and "welfare
education" (*Erziehungsfürsorge* and *Fürsorgeerziehung* in
German) are not always well differentiated; the two phrases
are often used indiscriminately, the one for the other. We
shall therefore do well to hold fast to this distinction: educational welfare work is a general concept, whereas welfare
education is a particular branch of educational welfare work.

Any retraining activity which sets for itself the task of
dealing with juveniles who have become wayward and criminal, and of leading them back toward social integration, falls

"Kann der Jugendliche straffällig werden? Ist das Jugendgericht eine
Lösung?" *Zeitschrift für psychoanalytische Pädagogik*, 8:77-95, 1934.

*Editor's Note:* The subject of this present work, revised and enlarged for the
*Zeitschrift für psychoanalytische Pädagogik*, was treated by the author
for the first time in a lecture delivered in Vienna, October, 1924, at a
session of the Central Agency for Youth Welfare and the Protection of the
Child [*Zentralstelle für Kinderschutz und Jugendfürsorge*], within the frame-
work of the proceedings concerning a reform of the penal law for juveniles.
A second, expanded lecture on the same theme was delivered in Paris,
July, 1928, at the Conference of Welfare Work and Social Policy. It was
published under the title "The Juvenile Court: Is It a Solution?" (in
English) in the *Revue Internationale de l'Enfant*, 9:195, 1930. The *Union
Internationale de Secours aux Enfants* made use of this paper in one of its
own written Inquiries, and also transmitted it to the Committee on the
Protection of the Child of the League of Nations.

within the realm of educational welfare work. But if such minors are committeed to a reform institution, properly speaking, we are engaging in welfare education.

Prophylactic measures for the prevention of delinquency and criminality among juveniles were not considered. The minor who found himself in danger of becoming wayward did not arouse interest. Only when he became dangerous to society at large—in other words, when he had become guilty of acts of commission or omission that stand in contradiction to the prevailing norms—society started dealing with him. It is the "criminal" who attracted attention, the juvenile criminal no more than the adult. Both were dangerous, and both had to be rendered harmless.

Legislation and penal practice made no essential distinction between the two categories: "Anybody who had attained the age of fourteen was treated exactly like an adult. Punishment was meted out to him, and what became of him thereafter was nobody's concern" (Altmann, 1929).

A penal code as comparatively recent as that of Empress Maria Theresa, promulgated on December 3, 1768, allows that young children, who are closer to the age of fourteen than seven, may under certain circumstances be made to suffer the death penalty. It is only in early childhood before the age of seven, or in the case of young boys and girls who are closer to the age of seven than to fourteen, that a verdict of execution by hanging cannot be carried out.

Juvenile and adult transgressors of the law were locked up and put to work together in the same penitentiaries. A youth was then exposed to all the damaging influence of his mates, the adult criminals. The agencies of penal jurisdiction at first formulated the demand that the juveniles should be segregated in their own wards and that they should be given separate living space, especially at night. Though these requirements were fulfilled, very little could be achieved thereby. Work was still performed in common by adults and minors, and despite the strictest supervision during working and rest hours, one could not prevent evil consequences.

Later on, when the juvenile sections—or correctional wards—obtained their own wings or buildings within the prison, the work was distributed in such a way that it was no longer performed in common by adults and minors; and yet it proved impossible to hinder completely the mingling of juveniles and grownups. It was thought that the segregation would solve the problem entirely. But the prison guards and supervising personnel continued to treat the juveniles just as before and the same old spirit prevailed. All this seemed normal at that time, for there was as yet no inclination to consider the youthful criminal from a psychological angle. Civil servants from the Department of Justice were appointed directors of "Reformatories" (the name given to the new institutions), while former noncommissioned officers of the army became supervisors, who did not differ from those employed in the prisons for adult criminals. It was left to chance alone whether such supervisors had the proper qualifications for the new job. As a matter of fact, they were often ill-fitted for their task; but much of the criticism which contemporary observers leveled at the supervising personnel would have been aimed more deservedly at the defects of the system itself.

The success so confidently expected from the new institutions failed to materialize; the percentage of recidivists among the released juvenile ex-prisoners remained disproportionately high. This fact, and the method of treating the youthful inmates as if they were convicts, finally brought the reform institutions into disrepute. The need for drastic changes was recognized; but the line of development had been set and improvements could be introduced only within narrowly determined limits. At the helm of the reformatories, the civil servants from the Department of Justice were replaced by teachers, and a regular scholastic curriculum was introduced. This of course required the services of schoolteachers. The activity of the teachers was, however, restricted to the field of actual schoolteaching, while the supervision of the pupils remained in the hands of former noncommissioned officers. Until the promulgation of the law establishing the Juvenile Court, there occurred few changes. The teachers acquired influence over the activities of the pupils outside lesson hours, and their position was gradually recognized as above that of the supervisors. Under pressure from the growing interest in public welfare, which was spreading and becoming more and more sentimental, reformatories had to change their name to "Training Schools"; yet the inner structure of these so-called educational institutions remained more or less the same as before. One illustration: in our own way, we had been working in Ober-Hollabrunn (Aichhorn, 1925) with pupils falling in the category of welfare education wards, whereas in the "reform institutions" the inmates were still being castigated with rods and locked up in solitary confinement according to an official statute which prescribed so many strokes for each kind of transgression. During a visit to one of these reformatories, the director told us the following example of "progress" in his institution: "I myself prescribe in each case the exact number of strokes of the rod; but first, the culprit is submitted to medical examination, so as to establish whether he is physically strong enough to bear the punishment. Also, I am present at the performance of the whipping, so as to make sure that the supervisor does not commit any excesses."

There are today certain countries who pride themselves on the enactment of special laws concerning juvenile delinquents. Their legislation makes due allowance for the immaturity of childhood and youth and also takes into account the common experience that penalties do not always achieve the hoped-for results, and that other means of training are required to complement the function of punishment.

We, the educational welfare workers, who are no longer content with mere rationalizations, and who are now trained to seek out the unconscious tendencies which lead to waywardness and criminal actions, find it natural and interesting to investigate the unconscious motives of the legislator himself. We try to distinguish in his work those elements which indicate a higher comprehension of the subject from those elements which are rooted in the legislator's own emotional attitudes. To point out merely one aspect of the question: We would be happy if legislation concerning juvenile delinquency freed itself from the exclusive wish to protect society against the youthful lawbreaker. If the laws would take into account the hard fact that both waywardness and criminality originate in psychic illness, that it is in our power today to heal the illness, further therapeutic methods could and should be found. In other words: we should not "reform," but bring *remedy*.

When, for example, a young thief stops stealing as the result of an appropriate punishment, society at large is satisfied and pacified. But the question of whether he himself has been cured falls outside the competence of applied penal law. Yet there exists a symptomless phase, or condition, in the development of wayward youth, wherein there is no visible manifestation of delinquency, and no criminal acts are committed since the punishment was meted out—the delinquency has become latent.[1]

But latent delinquency cannot be cured either by keeping asocial youth in a penal institution, or by applying to him the educational means—reward and punishment—that are at the disposal of ordinary pedagogy.

Even the Austrian legislation concerning juvenile delinquency which was passed on January 1, 1929 displays unintentionally in its very preamble those strongly affective motives which turn society against the youthful lawbreaker. The first paragraph reads ". . . and the opinions about the right methods by which a proper respect for law and order might be infused in their hearts" (the hearts of youthful lawbreakers). These words betray the will of society to remain unperturbed and to coerce the lawbreaker into becoming a law-abiding citizen. Otherwise, this passage in the preamble would read differently; it might be worded: "to lead the

---

[1] For the distinction of manifest versus latent delinquency, see Aichhorn (1932).

youthful lawbreakers toward a recognition of the existing legal order."

The preamble states further:

> However—and today there is no longer any disagreement on this point—the said task does not consist in causing the youthful lawbreaker to suffer a penalty in requital for the harm which he has inflicted, through his action, to both the legal order and to the victim; rather it consists in saving the juvenile delinquent from himself, in providing him with that power of moral restraint which he lacks, in protecting him for his own sake as well as for the sake of society from the danger of becoming a slave to his harmful tendencies—those tendencies the existence of which has been disclosed by the act which he has committed. Punishment, in certain circumstances, may also contribute to such purpose, on condition that the method of punishment and the way of applying the penalty are consistent with the educational aim.
>
> Thus understood, punishment does not stand in contradiction to pedagogy; it merely represents one of the means which may be used for the purpose of education.

The principle of retribution has been renounced, yet it does not seem, at this time, that one is prepared to dispense with punishment as a means of "reforming" the wayward. Now punishment is motivated as a method of education; apparently, such a motivation is necessary in order to answer the scruples of society, which wants to feel it has fulfilled its duty toward juveniles who have committed offenses against the law.

But we may well ask the question whether punishment, as an educational means (see Chapter 4), has not acquired a new significance in the light of our present knowledge; and whether, therefore, we should continue to view it in the generally accepted manner.

We have learned from psychoanalysis that in every case of delinquency unconscious motives are at work; and that such unconscious psychic processes are not only important, but in most instances decisively so. This discovery must necessarily

alter, in a fundamental way, our attitude toward punishment
as a means of education, and perhaps more generally toward
the imposition of penalties. A few specifically chosen examples
will suffice to give the reader an over-all idea of the part
played by the unconscious in various types of antisocial
manifestation.

A fifteen-year-old girl is doing well in school, but is lazy,
inattentive and untidy, and is in danger of being committed
to an institution, because her parents are afraid that their
household helper will complain to the police about the girl.
The reason is the following. The child was asked to put her
school things in order; she sorted out her books, papers, and
other belongings on the floor and on the bed. But, in her
usual way, she started this job with a flourish only to leave it
undone: the books and notebooks were scattered all over the
place and she went away in the middle of her work. The
household helper had to put things in order. When the
child came back, she started complaining that the helper
"had managed to disarrange everything again!" Without
unfriendliness the woman tried to appease the child, but the
girl worked herself into such a fury that she hurled a drink-
ing glass at the helper, hitting her on the nose and causing a
wound which had to be treated medically. According to her
mother's report, the child loses every shred of self-control in
her fits of ill-temper: she blusters, shouts, kicks, tears up the
clothes and notebooks of her brothers and sisters, throws any
object within her reach at the persons who happen to be in
the room, spills ink, breaks glasses and crockery, and behaves
with incredible wickedness and violence. Several times she
went so far as to threaten those present with a knife; but
each time they succeeded in tearing the weapon away from
her grip, so that it was not possible to establish whether she
would really have hurt anyone.

Let us suppose, for the sake of argument, that the scene
would actually have resulted in a complaint to the police.
The juvenile court would have had to take up the case, if
for no other reason, because of the wound inflicted upon the

helper. The inquiry would then have shown—as we ourselves were to establish—that the family circumstances were decent, that the child's brothers and sisters, brought up in the same environment, were behaving normally, and that the girl had already undergone a psychiatric examination with negative results. As to the interrogation of the child before the court, it could only have strengthened the impression about her bad disposition: self-centered, evil, extraordinarily aggressive. Her commitment to a training school would have been a foregone conclusion.

Instead of taking such a drastic decision, we submitted the child to a "psychoanalysis for delinquents."[2] This analysis made it plain that she was living in a continuous, though quite unconscious, state of anxiety. It would lead us too far if we tried to present all the determinants of this condition. It is enough if we see that this child feels herself temporarily relieved from anxiety whenever she gains the upper hand during a conflict with grownups. The violent fits of aggressiveness express, first of all, a desire to startle the adults. But there is also an unconscious wish that is less distorted: the wish to be overwhelmed by the grownups, so as to be placed again in the former situation of anxiety. The psychoanalysis of the child, which uncovered the relationship that had created her unconscious feelings of guilt and need for punishment, resulted in her cure. The girl was able to remain with her family even during the psychoanalytic treatment.

Another case: a thirteen-year-old boy had repeatedly been committed to various institutions, since the age of ten, because he had been guilty of chronic thieving. His first thefts, within the family, took place seven years ago. Although his mother used to punish him severely, his pilferings had become more and more frequent. When he started stealing outside the home, he was put into a reformatory. From there he was taken back temporarily by his family, because of the

---

[2] Aichhorn means psychoanalytic treatment of the child by a child analyst.

letters he had written home, in which he implored for forgiveness and promised to improve his ways. But he had
relapsed each time. In the reform institutions, despite severest
treatment, no improvement in his behavior took place.

The boy was brought to the clinic when all the previous
efforts had failed. He was well on his way to become a criminal. He was a good-looking boy, with rather passive, feminine
traits of character, and the typical disposition of a swindler.
He was born shortly after the death of his father, and was
smothered by his hysterical mother with an overflow of
tenderness. The two lived alone for nearly four years, when
the woman married again, and then the child had to share
the tender love of his mother with a stepfather.

During treatment, the unconscious relationships were made
conscious, and a successful cure was effected. We know that
if we relate here just one of the unconscious motives, this
does not alone suffice to furnish a proof; but it may well be
of interest even to those readers who are not psychoanalysts,
as an illustration of those unconscious factors which contribute to the manifestation of waywardness.

The entry of a husband and stepfather into the house had
changed the attitude of the mother toward the child. It was
disclosed only during our treatment that the mother used to
show much more tenderness after each punishment inflicted
on the boy for an act of misbehavior; he had come to behave
worse and worse, precisely in order to recapture those tender
motherly attentions which had formerly been his. According
to the youth's recollections, it was his mother who had
punished him for his first theft (money taken from her purse),
though immediately after the punishment she hugged and
kissed him, in a way quite reminiscent of the days before
the advent of the stepfather. The child had gone through the
same experience on the occasion of his second and third
thefts. He was unconsciously guided along the way which
resulted in recapturing his mother's tenderness. He became a thief largely because he expected and desired unconsciously to be punished for his guilt by his mother, and

then to be forgiven by her in an endearing manner. These phenomena of delinquency serve to demonstrate the "secondary gain" of delinquent manifestations.

A twelve-year-old boy is sent by his school to the child guidance clinic, because since the age of eight he has been in the habit of running away each year at springtime; he often remains away for many days, until caught and brought home by the police. As we wish to know whether this case of waywardness is not determined at least in part by organic causes, we have the child examined first of all psychiatrically. The result of this examination neither confirms nor excludes the presence of an "organically determined urge to wander," or of an epileptic twilight state. We are therefore thrown back upon our own methods of finding out what the trouble is. We learn from the boy's mother that he was born out of wedlock; that he had been brought up in the country until the age of six by his maternal grandmother; and that when he reached school age, he was sent back to his own mother; who had meanwhile married. His mother's economic circumstances were bad. The boy found himself living in a family of four, lodging in a single room and kitchen. When asked about the child's behavior, the mother answered that he was uncommonly withdrawn, had no friends, and would sit sullenly in a corner, often for hours. His school report showed him to be poor; he was held back twice. He sits in the classroom, staring vacantly and learning nothing. Yet the intelligence test, which we checked ourselves, shows a normal I.Q.

All the detailed factors which had to be uncovered before the boy was cured can hardly be explained here. It is clear that this child must have suffered a bad shock in his sixth year, when he was torn away from a beloved grandmother and a congenial rustic environment to be transplanted into a crowded, dull, unsympathetic proletarian milieu, where no one cared for him. The child continued to live, in his imagination, the joyful life which he had experienced in his grandmother's house, and locked himself more and more in this imaginary world, as the reality became less and less pleasurable. On the other hand, the practical demands of everyday life required that he give up his fantasy, that he push it out of his consciousness. Yet it remained powerful enough to make him a misfit in his environment. But each spring, when sunshine came back, there would be an upsurge of imagination welling up into the consciousness of the child; then he would go away, for he must seek and find the lost beauty of his earlier childhood. During his treatment, he said to us once: "Now I know why I was always running away. When there was a sunset, and a peal of church bells, which were so wonderful, I simply *had* to get them back."

A woman comes to visit a welfare training school with her seventeen-year-old son, whom she wants to leave at the school. The reason: "For some time now, my son has been taking a kitchen knife to bed with him. This he explains to me by saying that 'Very soon now, I shall stab this dog,'" meaning his own father. I shall certainly not complain to the police, and I am quite sure the boy is not mad. But he hates his father so strongly, that I am really afraid something dreadful might happen. Therefore, I must put my son in a reform school." When the youth was submitted to a "psychoanalysis for delinquents," the gaps in his recollection were filled in gradually until one day he said: "I have the feeling that daddy once wanted to strangle my mother." During the next few months of treatment, there emerged some verbal descriptions which made this feeling more explicit; for instance: "I was not yet going to school; I am standing up in my crib and I observe my parents who are lying in bed; I can see how father is strangling my mother, while she tries to resist him and groans." Such memories show us that in his early childhood this boy had overheard his parents at night and had interpreted their behavior, in his childish way, as an act of aggression by his father against his mother. We also learn that his loathing for his father began to develop in this period, and that it expressed itself at first in extreme naughtiness at the father's expense. As seen from the viewpoint of early childhood, he was merely siding with his mother against a "brutal" father who threatened her. But even after he had revealed to us these fragmentary recollections, they did not interconnect to form a coherent picture in his own mind. The counselor who treated him asked him: "You are already seventeen years old; don't you realize now what your father and mother were doing?" The youth was so startled that he could only stammer out: "My God, am I dumb!" The further behavior of the boy made it plain that one could now attempt to bring him and his parents together. They were invited to visit the institution, and the very first meeting brought about a full reconciliation, with much hugging, kissing, and crying of all three participants. Two years later, the welfare worker who had been in charge of the treatment happened to meet the boy's mother. She told him: "When I think that I brought my son to your institution in order to prevent him from murdering his own father, all this seems today like a bad dream to me. You cannot imagine how the two of them, father and son, hang together; how they understand each other. . . . It would almost be my turn to become jealous!"

One may well imagine what would have happened if the youth had not been removed from his family at the right time: his hatred might well overcome his inner resistance, and he might have murdered his father! He would then have stood trial as a patricide. Neither an inquiry into his antecedents, nor a psychiatric examination ordered by the court, nor the most thoroughgoing interrogation of the youthful criminal, would have been able to bring to light the true motives of the deed.

It is also clear from the relationship described that the youth would have shown no feelings of repentance before the court. The unconscious motives of his action are not accessible to his conscious judgment, as a consequence he himself cannot evaluate them. But repentance may set in only when the conscious motives of an action come to be regarded as bad by the person concerned. This is probably the reason why youthful criminals are so often accused of displaying "callousness" before the attorney, the court, the public: their attitude is really misunderstood, and they are thus not allowed any possible "extenuating circumstances."

The few examples given above are enough to prove the insufficiency of those premises upon which legislators have based their codes for juvenile delinquents.

In what follows, we shall try to discover the most general causal relations; but we are aware that it takes much more than the discovery of causes to find a solution of the problem itself.

The solution must be sought in another direction than that which has been followed so far. This should stimulate other minds to work in the psychological field in order to prepare ground for future legislation. We wish to make here two introductory observations.

We do not rely on the data of criminal statistics. They cannot give us any insight into those causal relations which we seek to discover. This discovery depends upon psychological considerations, which in turn are based on experience acquired in the course of our educational work with juvenile delinquents and criminals. We see the facts in the light of the psychoanalytic method; that is, we exclude all that which is accidental in the realm of the psyche; we take the unconscious into account; and, moreover, we consider crime and manifestation of waywardness as a single though complex resultant of psychic forces which flow into each other, or complement each other, or work antagonistically against each other.

We are not unaware that the various attempts to find the causes of delinquency and criminality differ widely. There are those who follow the sociological way; they seek the original cause in the environment of the juvenile, and trace it back to economic and social conditions; in other words, they regard causality as something bound up entirely with external factors. Then there are the others, who limit their horizon to the individual and look for the cause in the criminal himself. To them, the important point is the constitutional character of the criminal.

While both schools of research have to recognize the fact that there are always exogenous as well as endogenous factors at work in crime and waywardness, the researchers of each school nevertheless remain faithful to their fundamental opinions when it comes to explanation. We do not intend to accept either one of the two standpoints; we shall rather start from the individual and consider how the influences of the surrounding world act upon him.

Every child is an original being, whose individuality is determined by the quality, the amount, and the mutual combination of hereditary factors; furthermore, this original being is possessed necessarily with an urge to express his own congenital character. But he is born into a given environment, which in its turn represents a decisive factor. Very often, the child is coerced into adopting an attitude that stands in contradiction to his disposition.

If the child nevertheless manages to fit himself into his surroundings, or if he succeeds in responding without too much inner conflict to the demands made on him, so that he finds his bearings and later on accepts the rules of society, then such a development will be taken for granted by the adults as well as by society at large, especially when the child happens not to cause particular difficulties in his upbringing and does not become a nuisance to the grownups. We need not concern ourselves here with such children. But there are many who do not fit in so easily and do not give up as a matter of course their own original ways of developing. (In this discussion, disregard those who are intellectually deficient.) These difficult children resist their upbringing, they disturb the routine, they are obnoxious in their own homes. The resultant faulty development leads sometimes toward delinquency and crime—that is, to such a glaring conflict with law and order that society has to take defensive measures, no doubt, rightly so. Yet there is no question but that the means which society employs today for its defense are not the right means. It would be more economical for both society and the individual if one would try to cure the delinquent instead of reforming him.

Let us try to get a clearer picture of how the adults go about their task of turning the growing generation into "useful members of the community." It is in our time that the problem of childhood and the child's development has become a matter of particular importance to parents and to society at large. During the last forty years, the position of the child within the family has undergone a considerable shift, at least in certain sections of the population. Formerly, it was the father who came first, followed by the mother, with the children trailing behind. But now the order is almost the reverse. Nevertheless, the parents' attitude toward the child does not yet correspond to the child's dominant position. The treatment of children does not serve their genuine needs. Apparently, it is not for his own sake that the child has become the chief person within the family; the preference he now enjoys is due much rather to unconscious motives, as he represents a suitable object for the discharge of his parents' emotions. As to the causes which led to such an evolution, they deserve a separate investigation.

The child and his upbringing have always been an emotional concern of his parents: this is something which, to all appearances, cannot be changed. But is is easy to detect that inasmuch as the parents engage today more often than formerly in discussions about problems in child rearing or about aims and means of education, their own affective relations to the child are also strengthened thereby. This, however, works out to the child's detriment. For as the emotional attachment of the educators (the parents) to the object of education (the child) becomes more intense, their capacity to understand clearly the child's genuine needs decrease. (A typical case is that of the only child.)

In sections of the population where there has been no change in the child's position within the family, one finds other obstacles in the way of a favorable development of the child. The parents follow their own occupations and are absorbed more or less completely by their daily worries; or, as it often happens, they are so exhausted by the struggle for existence that they sink into a state of dull resignation and indifference at home. There is hardly a trace left of the tender feelings which once prevailed in the relations between husband and wife. Mostly, they live side by side rather than together; they quarrel openly in front of the children; or they nurse their grudges until there prevails that sultry atmosphere in which an explosion may come at any minute. The daily routine revolves around practical problems that have little in common with the question of the child's personality and development.

In the many years of our own direct experience in dealing with wayward youth, we have not met with a single case of crime or delinquency where the family background was wholesome. In countless instances, it was quite obvious that the parents did not live harmoniously together; in others, such parental differences remained hidden, only to be revealed after a thoroughgoing investigation.

In these circumstances, so unfavorable to his normal development, a child requires a particularly robust constitution to grow up as a person capable in his turn of leading a life of satisfaction and happiness, within a social community where he fits in and where he contributes to the increase of economic and cultural goods. Whenever such constitutional robustness is lacking, it is highly probable that the child will develop as an antisocial person.

The task of rearing children fails very often without the public's becoming aware of it. Indeed, public opinion takes notice only of the more glaring cases of failure. As to statistics, they take cognizance solely of those instances where the failure is so complete as to require additional measures for society's protection. If it were possible to set up statistics concerning successes in rearing children, it would become obvious that the statistical analysis of crimes does not convey anything about the extent of failures. There are huge numbers of people who spend their whole lives, more or less joyless, drab lives, without any personal success, as a result of miscarried upbringing; but these people cannot be sized up by any statistical method. They can be observed, however, and are noticed by the attentive observer.

If we want to take up such considerations as may lead us ultimately to a new and different approach toward youth turned criminal, we must start from certain preliminary observations concerning the general task of bring up children.

Child rearing should never become an emotional activity; it must always remain a conscious endeavor aiming at the transformation of the child, an instinctual being, into a civilized person. Viewed superficially, education could therefore be conceived as a perpetual struggle against the child's instinctual wishes. The task of the educator would then consist in building a dam to hold back these impulses of the child. The success of such an upbringing would be measured by its ability to suppress the instinctual desires, at first through external coercion, and later on through the pressure of an inner power to be developed in the child himself. But such a condition creates a state of constant danger for the child. The child's authority, either external or internal, which sets up prohibitions, may be overwhelmed by instinctual storms, thus clearing the way toward delinquency. On the other hand, if the parent, or teacher, makes only demands which aim at restriction rather than suppression of the instincts, and if he endeavors to shape these demands in a manner acceptable to the child—indeed, there should always exist an adequate relation between a prohibition and the instinctual desire which it prohibits—then it may become possible to lead the child eventually toward a position of self-control, where he should be able to restrict the fulfillment of his instinctual wishes. Instead of bringing about the suppression of a wish, he would renounce an instinctual gratification, at least on its more primitive level; the instinctual urge would then become manageable, and could be diverted toward culturally more valuable aims.

It is well known that in pedagogical practice we have at our disposal only two means of producing in the child a tendency toward instinctual restriction: namely, the fear of punishment (see Chapter 4) and the granting of a substitutive pleasure in the guise of the tutor's affection. The parent or teacher must realize that every educational action exerts a pressure upon the child, the need for which the child cannot at first grasp. He therefore quite understandably tries to fend it off; for, indeed, the prohibition which restricts the instinct does not abolish the instinctual impulse: it only robs the wish of its natural satisfaction. But the urge of the unfulfilled instinctual demand will force the child to react one way or the other. At first he will try to render the prohibition ineffectual. If he does not succeed in this, then he will try to circumvent the prohibition.

Let us now observe how children react, in many different ways, to prohibitions that demand from them a restriction of instincts. We may distinguish several kinds of behavior.

Despite the prohibition, the child immediately yields to his instinctual impulse, until satisfaction is obtained. The prohibition has remained altogether ineffectual.

Another type of behavior: the instinctual impulse is still able to overcome the prohibition entirely; but the tempo of the instinctual gratification becomes modified; it is slowed down. Such reaction is observable mostly in very young children, when a prohibition interferes with their minor bodily bad habits (such as nose picking), bad habits which to them are pleasurable.

Yet another type: the prohibition may act so strongly that the child must take a roundabout way in order to reach somehow the satisfaction of his instinctual desire. He tries begging, wheedling, cajoling, insisting on his wish, until the grownups are so tired out that they yield, and he can reach his instinctual aim without being declared bad. In most cases, parents do not realize that their children strive in this way to bypass an established prohibition, and that they are often successful.

A different type occurs when the prohibition is felt to be so unpleasant that the child rebels against it. He grumbles, cries, shouts, sulks, etc. (A more particular way out, with which we shall not concern ourselves here, is taking refuge in illness.)

It requires many unsuccessful attempts before a child resigns himself to giving up the discharge of all those elements in the urges that press outward; and until he reaches the stage when those defensive mechanisms are set in motion which psychoanalysis has made familiar to us under the title of "repression." To be sure, the setting up of such mechanisms is facilitated by the fact that the experience of the child's forebears has not remained ineffective (primal repression).

Repression removes from consciousness the impelling force of unsatisfied instinctual wishes; and therefore the desires lose their tormenting character, for now he has forgotten his instinctual wish. We shall not examine here the interesting problem of unsatisfied instinctual impulses which go on working as unconscious forces and may become the source of cultural achievements. We are concerned now with quite another form in which a repressed desire can externalize itself. We know it all too well in the normal child as "badness." (This expression, as used currently in Austria, conveys a somewhat more stringent meaning than that of the merely "naughty" child.)

The child's bad behavior is interpreted by parents and pedagogues as the sign of an upbringing which has not been entirely successful; therefore, an effort is made immediately to eradicate this "badness." Conversely, the result of a proper upbringing is considered to be a well-behaved, "good" child. And, in fact, with normal children, one succeeds frequently in bringing about such a result, that is, to make the child well-behaved, be it at the cost of great pleasure.

But the question arises: are expressions of badness rightly interpreted when they happen to be of this kind? Or is another interpretation not equally possible? Let us assume that the bad behavior is a child's reaction to the educational measures themselves: in this case, the child's badness must be considered as a form of rebellion, and we should conclude logically that such rebellion is based upon an aggressive tendency in the child. This aggressiveness, in its turn, can strive toward no other goal but to reach, in spite of every obstacle, the primitive satisfaction of an instinctual urge, or to cause unpleasantness to the educator and to take revenge upon him, thus netting once more a pleasure gain for the child. Between the bad behavior and the measures prescribed, one could postulate a relationship which might be formulated in the following way. The quantitative amounts of bad behavior express the fluctuations of counterpressure in the child caused by the stresses of his upbringing. This would furnish us with a kind of manometer, represented by manifestations of badness. If only we had learned to make the proper observations beforehand, we could make use of this "manometer" for checking our own educational actions and adapting them to the individual character of our pupils. (Of course, our remarks do not apply to the well-known expressions of "bad" behavior on the part of neurotic children.)

Let us go back once more to the currently accepted notions about a child's badness. These notions do not take into account the following fact: in a well-behaved, "good" child, the aggressive tendency remains unsatisfied and must therefore seek some other outlet. When the adults have succeeded in bringing up their charge as a well-behaved child, they have of course obtained a result satisfactory for their own comfort, but at the cost of suppressing the child's manifestations of badness. They thus deprive themselves of the most important means of observation of the effects of their methods of rearing. Nor can they gauge the burdens imposed upon the child by the very process of education. The "manometer" has been smashed. With it those relations have been obliterated that bind certain phenomena of nervous conditions in a child or certain manifestations of waywardness to the child's primitive rebellion, a rebellion which had been locked out of its original channels of expression.

Now if we return to the conception that badness in a child represents his revolt against the power of his upbringing, then we must likewise interpret such manifestations as the most primitive form of asociality. If rebellion is a form of delinquency, its content is aggression. We are inclined to accept the opinion that the content of the various expressions of crime and delinquency consists in sheer aggressiveness. This means that all the manifold varieties of asocial acts and behavior differ among themselves only in form. These various forms correspond to individual experiences, to different types of resistance reaction (either simple or complex) against training measures, and to the mosaic of identifications originating in earliest childhood. Thus considered, the waywardness and criminality of juveniles should be interpreted merely as a consequence of crises in upbringing which come from retardation in the child's development, or regression to an earlier stage. Without examining any particular expressions of delinquency, we may learn from two features present in the make-up of each and every delinquent and criminal, and point consistently to a discrepancy between the actual age of the person and the phase of development he has reached. These two features are the following: the presence of an irrepressible need for immediate gratification of instincts, and the fact that such moral rules as are valid in society have no compelling force for the individual concerned.

The categorical imperative which makes it quite impossible for an adult social being to act otherwise than in a social manner, and which towers as a sharply critical observer above the acting "ego," whom it likes or dislikes, praises or condemns, while providing also a model and expression of what the ego should be, is something entirely lacking in the wayward and the criminal. The child possesses in his "ego" a kernel of this critical function; the normal youth has it already in a partially developed form, which may be temporarily stultified, however, by paroxysms in the instinctual urges. But in delinquent juveniles it is permanently subjugated by such impulses. This accounts for the failure of the delinquent to reach that developmental phase which would otherwise normally correspond to his age level; or, in different words, it accounts for the failure of training to accomplish its task, whatever the reasons.

Society cannot leave unnoticed this failure in the behavior of delinquents and criminals. In fact, society resorts to measures of two different kinds: welfare education and penal prosecution. We are not concerned at this moment with welfare education. But it remains to examine whether the juvenile delinquent, be he child or youth, may become guilty in the sense in which guilt is defined by law. The two forms of guilt which are known in law, namely, *dolus* (ill intent) and *culpa* (negligence), do not seem to us to be applicable in the domain of these crises in the rearing of children. Furthermore, society's sense of justice demands that punishment should overtake the true culprit. But the condemnation of children and young people according to penal law does not hit the guilty party according to our concept. Penal law throws the responsibility upon a juvenile who is himself the innocent victim of unsuccessful rearing, without bothering to find out the causes of this failure. It should be admittted, of course, that whatever the precise circumstances, no true culprit can be found in most such cases, and no one person exists who could be actually considered as guilty. One usually has to deal with vicissitudes brought about by chance, and there is no one who could be made responsible for them. Nevertheless, we are of the opinion that such circumstances do not justify society in singling out the innocent victim, the wayward youth, on the shallow ground that it is in him and through him that other people's defects are exposed, and their errors brought unpleasantly to our attention.

We dare assert that what the juvenile lawbreaker needs most of all is an opportunity to make up for his lack of proper training; and that such opportunity can be provided through welfare education, but not through penal sanctions. Our assertion is not in the least invalidated by the fact that welfare retraining, at the present stage of its development, is still unable to render legal punishment superfluous. It is merely a question of time until we reach the stage wherein the penal condemnation of juvenile lawbreakers will appear unnecessary. The same idea may be expressed in another way. New legislation will not accomplish reform of the delinquent; on the contrary, any such legislation must be rendered obsolete by progress in retraining youth.

One cannot prevent society from seeking protection against the youthful transgressor. But one must concede that the juvenile delinquent is entitled to hold society responsible for letting him grow up as a lawbreaker. When society appoints the judge of the tribunal dealing with juvenile delinquency as an attorney for the entire community, then the juvenile delinquent has a right to be represented by an attorney of his own. It was Reicher (1908) who stated: "I contest the right of the punitive power of the State to take action, before the State has fulfilled those duties which pertain to its own welfare function." When the laws regarding juvenile delinquency contain regulations which claim to take into account the peculiarities of the youthful character, and yet in their entire structure show that each regulation has been formulated to satisfy the emotional attitude of society, then we may only conclude that the legislation represents at best a compromise; a compromise reached at the expense of those who have already been wronged grievously enough by society itself.

It is not absolutely necessary, however, to wait until the time when welfare education will have become entirely adequate. It would be possible, in the near future, to do away with a considerable number of penal regulations in the codes for juvenile delinquents, if only the proper authorities were to interpret the word "judgment" in the sense of "understanding" or "diagnosis" instead of "verdict" or "condemnation."

To condemn is the business of the judge applying the penal law; but to determine the correct diagnosis in cases as complex as those that come up in courts for juvenile delinquents is something a single individual is not capable of doing. The penal judge would hardly be expected to fulfill this duty; but certainly it could be entrusted to a custodial judge, or better still, to a judge presiding over a juvenile court, and able to work together with the physician, the psychoanalyst, the remedial educator, the specialist of welfare education, the welfare worker and his female aids—in brief, with all those who provide the data needed for a proper diagnosis and who can carry out the measures prescribed. One should withdraw the youthful lawbreaker from the jurisdiction of penal tribunals, and hand him over to such an authority which might be constituted as an "educational high court."

Obviously, we do not suppose that such an educational high court would immediately be in a position to handle all youthful lawbreakers in a way acceptable to welfare education. This would be impossible for lack of adequate facilities, nor could one easily improvise the necessary facilities. But an educational high court should be something else: this court should embody the idea that juvenile delinquency courts should not represent a final point in the evolution, that we are concerned not with consolidating the tribunal and developing its code for a long time to come, but that we are engaged in furthering a development in a different direction. In brief, the educational high court must act as the germ cell of re-education.

We must admit that the suggestion of removing the youthful lawbreaker from the competence of penal jurisdiction and of handing him over to the authority of a juvenile court would have been more acceptable in the period before the present trend had had time to set in, that is, the trend toward penal legislation for juveniles. We are aware of the very great difficulties which will have to be overcome before such a court can be set up, even theoretically, as to its membership, its public and legal position, its sphere of activity, its limits in respect to the police and to penal jurisdiction, etc. We also know that such a tremendous and complex question as this one cannot be dealt with, even on a provisional basis, without thorough preliminary spadework of elucidation and negotiation with all the institutions and authorities involved. We would therefore be content if the foregoing suggestions were simply to provide a starting point for those who seek to solve the problem of how to treat the youthful lawbreaker.

# IV

## Reward or Punishment

## as a Means of Education?

A consensus has not yet been reached in regard to methods of rearing children. There are those who still argue in favor of severity, threat of punishment, and actual punishment; and those who speak up for mildness, kindness, and the premium of love. One cannot deny the fact that educational results are attained through punishment as well as through reward, while failure cannot be excluded by the use of either of these methods. "Severe" educators assert that the poorer results are due to mildness, whereas the "mild" educators make exactly the contrary claim. Unfortunately, there are no statistics concerning educational successes, which might show us that the one assertion is right and the other wrong.

Perhaps the following point has not been sufficiently considered: methods of rearing depend upon educational aims, or, in other words, upon the object of education, the child himself. They depend also upon general as well as particular circumstances which surround the educational work. The

"Lohn oder Strafe als Erziehungsmittel?" *Zeitschrift für psychoanalytische Pädagogik,* 5:273-285, 1931.

*Editor's Note:* Here the larger concept of *Erziehung* (upbringing, training, teaching) must be kept in mind.

considerations here presented are not a result of scientific inquiry, but rather a broad summary of theoretical reflections which emerge from practical experience. Our task shall have been fulfilled if we succeed in stimulating the reader, and encourage him to add new observations, or to qualify, rectify, or even refute our findings. In this way, we shall discover a number of facts which belong together. A methodical gathering of these bits of knowledge in a systematic unit should yield some new and well-founded conclusions, valuable for the entire discipline of pedagogy.

Anyone who brings up children does it with a certain intention, and cherishes the hope that they will develop in accordance with this expectation. Far from remaining passive, the parent or teacher intervenes actively in their development. Such intervention may be a well-considered action, or a merely instinctual manifestation; but in both cases, the activities are based upon some definite educational idea. This idea is always present, even though it is not always conscious. The educational idea becomes psychically effective as an educational wish. The aim of this wish we call the educational aim. However, that part of it which becomes conscious is the result of a compromise, a compromise with the unconscious portion of the educational aim. The attainment of this aim will be furthered, or hampered, or even rendered impossible, depending upon whether the conscious or unconscious tendencies which motivate the parents (or educators) happen to point in a single direction, or in more or less divergent or even opposite directions. Attainment of the educational aim may be hindered also by obstacles in the character of the child himself.

This can be verified by observing the behavior of parents during the process of bringing up their children, as well as the child's reactions to this behavior. The following examples illustrate this point.

A shrewd, unscrupulous businessman, bent on exploiting other people for his own profit, loves his son (allegedly) to the point of idolatry, and wants to have him brought up as a dispassionate, objective observer of life, if possible as an outright ascetic. The father tries to justify his educational aim by pointing out that by the time his son grows up, merchants will have become superfluous, because of major changes in the structure of society. The son is a physical weakling and is mentally retarded. We happen to know that this father had been a severely delinquent youth, who was forced to behave in a socially acceptable manner only through the utmost discipline. He never became a really social being; even now, he is merely disguising his antisocial feelings; he has actually found a hidden outlet for his sadistic and vindictive tendencies in the exercise of his own trade. In his conscious educational aim, this father has formulated a demand (seemingly based upon realistic considerations) that his child should become adjusted to a life which would not be luxurious. This "ascetic" demand allows him to satisfy his unconscious tendencies; it permits him to inflict upon his son those same unhappy conditions of childhood from which he himself had suffered, and to gratify his own sadism by tormenting his child.

This case shows how a conscious educational aim may be modified by unconscious interests. The next example will teach us how an unconscious tendency may influence the achievement of a "conscious" educational aim.

A mother demands from the tutor of her elder son that he should educate him to become an independent person, who accepts life gladly and finds joy in his work. She herself had failed to achieve this goal. At the time the educator takes over, the mama's boy is a worthless, scatterbrained, and utterly spoiled child, unable to profit by any teaching. Very soon the tutor decides to give up altogether, because the mother manages to frustrate all his efforts, including those aimed at achieving precisely what she herself had demanded.

While this mother consciously wants to see her boy develop as an able, self-reliant man, she is incapable of resisting her own unconscious trends which cause the entire educational work to fail. She cannot stand the means needed for a proper education of her son, because it would mean the end of his absolute dependence upon her.

Still another illustration: A woman marries a widower with two children, a one-year-old boy and a three-year-old girl. The woman conceives it her duty to be a perfect substitute mother for her stepchildren. She even renounces the idea of having children of her own. Yet she has to apply to a child guidance clinic, where she seeks advice because of difficulties encountered in the upbringing of the little girl. In the clinic, this woman reaffirms her resolution, and tells how she had decided not to have any children of her own, when the little boy (now three years old) showed signs of becoming entirely dependent upon her. He became extremely jealous of any other child with whom his stepmother might seem to be concerned, even momentarily. The difficulties with the girl, which began soon after her marriage, increased and became especially acute when the little boy died before reaching the age of four. The seven-year-old girl now began to quarrel with her stepmother, crying and yelling for hours at a stretch, so that the neighbors finally lodged a complaint against the woman for mistreating the child. Yet there is nothing which seems to the stepmother as mistreatment. In fact, the woman is quite unable to understand why this child should be so difficult to bring up. In her own opinion, she is treating Lucy (the little girl) even better than she had ever treated her baby brother, Herbert. She sits for hours at Lucy's side to make her eat her meals, for the girl is a very poor eater; she gives the greatest attention to the girl's outward appearance, and she makes dresses for her by hand, for she has no sewing machine, etc. Nevertheless, one perceives clearly from the stepmother's own accounts that she has unconsciously bestowed much more tenderness upon the little boy, now dead; and that she had brought him up in a more sensible way than his sister. She has repeatedly said to the little girl, "Why are you still alive while our poor Herbert had to die?" To her mind, this statement serves a definite educational purpose; when the counselor tries to explain that such a way of speaking to a child is quite inadmissible, he merely gets the following rejoinder: "Well, what else could I possibly tell her? How else could I impress upon her that she should behave better?"

The conscious educational aim pursued by this severely hysterical woman, who belongs to a Jewish lower-middle-class milieu, is quite in keeping with the ideals of this particular section in Vienna's population. Yet the aim cannot be reached, because of certain unconscious tendencies, or obstacles, that stand in the way. The little girl, Lucy, is being made responsible for her stepmother's sacrifice, the latter having given up the thought of bearing any children of her own. Death wishes are now preponderant. This is also shown quite clearly by the reaction of the child herself: her attitude is one of permanent defense; she stands up to her stepmother like an enemy, always ready to fight back.

The woman's success with the little boy, Herbert, is explainable by the mere fact that here the conscious and the unconscious educational aims did not counteract each other. The tendencies toward affection, both conscious and unconscious, were developing in the same direction.

One often finds insuperable obstacles in the child himself, so that the conscious educational aim cannot be reached, even when there are no unconscious tendencies in the parent that bar the way to the goal. For example: A part-time employee, who was unable to get training for a more intellectual profession because his parents could not afford it, lives in a state of acute dissatisfaction. When a son is born to him, he declares that the child should be brought up in such a way as to be able to succeed in the inevitable competition of life; namely, on terms more favorable than those experienced by his own father. The little boy is expected to learn much, even in his earliest childhood, and the father's demands increase during the boy's first years in school. "The youngster must become well educated," this is what the father keeps saying. He does not take into consideration that his son's limited intellectual capabilities do not allow such an education. And of course he does not grasp in the least why his own sincere, honest, and intensive efforts should remain so utterly fruitless. He does not realize that the child's difficulties stem in the main from the defensive attitude the child has adopted against his father's harsh and unyielding pressure. The attempt to satisfy, in the person of his son, his own frustrated superego ideal is doomed to fail because of the boy's insufficient capacity.

So far, we have clarified some points concerning the reciprocal interference of conscious and unconscious tendencies in the process of education and in the attainment of (or the failure to attain) the educational aim, but we have not touched upon the more basic problem of the educational goal itself.

Although the various goals which are set by educators may differ among themselves and often be irreconcilable, all of them are nevertheless dependent upon the values which parents and educators derive from their various ideologies, even if they are not aware of such a derivation.

For instance, within our own social order, saving money becomes a civic virtue, and theft is prohibited without exception. Parents and educators try to awaken in the child a taste for saving money. Special institutions, savings banks, undertake the same educational task for the entire community. But in a society which forbids the accumulation of private property, the money-saving man, a model of bourgeois virtue, must inevitably rate as a criminal.

As to theft, here is an extreme case which will serve to illustrate our point: Why don't we rob each other by stealing directly from each other's pocketbook? We may feel that our restraint is something which "goes without saying"; yet it is not in the least an instinctive thing: it is the product of an education which corresponds to a definite ideology. This ideology demands as a necessary part of our upbringing that we should be conditioned to accept and value other people's property as sacred, as untouchable. But the little child has no sense of property, and we ourselves had none during our childhood. Countless prohibitions had to be imposed upon us before the idea of property could become a matter of course, part and parcel of our own make-up. On the other hand, within a family of thieves, for instance, there rules another ideology, another scale of values, another educational goal: thieving is allowed outside one's own collectivity; and only he who lets himself be caught while stealing is considered a worthless person.

The word "criminal" means next to nothing by itself; it gains meaning only in relation to the transgression of certain definite social rules.

The parents (or educators) act under the spell of their own *Weltanschauung,* and they are emotionally convinced that their educational aims represent the only unconditionally valid ideal. Yet the fact is that every educational goal is founded upon a subjective set of values, which therefore may be "right" values only in a special, relative sense.

Even if we redefine an educational aim in scientific terms, we cannot alter the fact that every parent is attempting nothing else, in the last analysis, but to force the child into the rigid framework of such values as they recognize to be right. As soon as the child accepts this framework of values which has been forced upon him, his upbringing (education) is said to have been accomplished. But this same education is considered to have failed if the child, when grown to adulthood, accepts another scale of values than that established by his parents; or, while recognizing such standards in theory, does not live up to them.

People agree about values only in a limited way; each group possesses its own world, distinct from the world of the other groups; it lives within its own particular reality. What is common to all is merely an underlying foundation of basic —and mostly quite archaic—values. Upon this foundation there towers a vast and diverse structure, composed of partly common yet variously differentiated sets of values, yet comprising also in part values that are mutually incompatible and divergent. For every single group within a given society, its own particular reality has become far more important than that which underlies the life of the whole. It is hardly possible any more to set up an educational goal which would enjoy a measure of general validity; and because of that, we do not possess today, strictly speaking, any education capable of bringing up citizens for the State—despite all the efforts of those who stand up in defense of such an education, and who approve of the State as such. When all is said, the fact remains: every child is actually being educated for life within one particular reality, shaped in a way which is all its own. Therefore, the child's ability to adapt himself to reality is being trained for adaptation to only one given structure of reality. Consequently, he develops the capacity of renouncing or postponing certain pleasure gains, or even of accepting unpleasure, according to the requirements of the particular reality structure. Of course, the little child is not capable of these things; the younger he is, the more he strives to gain pleasure and to protect himself against unpleasure. For the child is anything but a "diminutive adult." He is an instinctual being, who has to be conditioned before he develops a desire to "grow up." To lift him from a level of instinctual existence to that of an adult person adapted to reality, the educator must apply a definite pedagogical treatment, capable of stimulating the pupil and inducing him to exert some inner effort. Whatever the set of values upon which the educational goal happens to rest, the immediate purpose of every pedagogy remains always a definite one: to arouse energies in the child which will produce a character which conforms with the educational goal, whatever this goal may be. These energies are generated by the imposition of prohibitions which restrict expression of the child's instincts. The greater the amount of energy used up for the purpose of building character, the more economical is the corresponding educational treatment.

There is still another way to describe the process of education. In the development of a child one may observe two different stages, which do not actually succeed each other but form two parallel and even interconnected phases. The child goes through the one phase of his own accord, while the other one is the result of the conscious influence of adults upon the child. The distinction is of course purely schematic.

At the first stage in his development, the child acquires a primitive capacity to adapt himself to an elementary reality; but this capacity is just barely sufficient for a naked self-assertion: a child tries to touch a hot oven out of sheer delight at the sight of fire. Of course he burns his fingers, and the severity of the burn is proportionate to the temperature of the oven and to the area of skin which comes in contact with it.[1] The child has harmed himself through his own initiative, and he becomes more cautious as a result of his suffering; there is no need for instruction or influence on the part of the adults. The child learns to avoid those pleasurable actions which lead to a collision with the elementary reality around him when these actions seem harmful because of the unpleasure in which they inevitably result. Between such pleasurable, yet harmful, experiences and the subsequent pain, there exists an unbreakable relationship, which extends also to the quantitative relation between pleasure and unpleasure. Through this entirely automatic process of pleasurable-unpleasurable experiences, the young child is forced to adapt himself to a primitive, elementary reality.

In the second phase of childhood experience, the grownup forces the child to accept his own, adult, standards, the set standards of the "real" world; this he does in order to prepare the child for life within a particular reality, characterized by a particular structure. In this context, therefore, the task of bringing up a child means the following: to transform a primitive ability of adaptation to reality into the capacity of adapting oneself to a different reality with its unique structure.

Now every educator is expected to perform his pedagogic task with ultimate success. His pupil is supposed to go

[1] For further examples, see Aichhorn (1925).

through the "second phase" of development according to established values, up to the point where he finally reaches the educational goal. But this would be possible only if the second phase were ruled by exactly the same causality as that which dominates the first phase; in other words, if here also, in this particularly shaped reality (with its prohibition against transgressions of a peculiar set of values), there always followed upon the forbidden experience of a pleasurable act, each time and automatically, the unavoidable and properly dosed unpleasure.

Yet such a natural and casual relationship does not exist in the second of the two phases. The child experiences quite often that upon a pleasurable transgression of the accepted norm there does not follow any unpleasure, or there follows an amount of unpleasure (too much, or too little, as the case may be), out of proportion to the transgression itself. The critical situation is not brought about—as in the first phase— by the pleasurable action. On the contrary, the transgression must first be perceived as such by the educator, before there can arise any "danger" to the guilty child. Because of that, there almost never arises the condition in which a proper dosage of unpleasure follows the transgression in a natural and inevitable way. Such a straightforward consequence is usually impeded by the attitudes of society and of the parent or pedagogue himself in regard to the means of education; or by the temperament, moods, precise emotional state of the educator, or the "smartness" of the child, and so forth. The circumstances which influence the actual dosage of unpleasure cannot possibly be shaped entirely in the right manner, our present situation being what it is. (In this respect, much would be gained by simply obtaining a psychoanalysis of each individual educator.) It would more likely be possible, just as it occurs in the "first phase," to connect in this second phase every pleasurable but prohibited action, quite automatically, with an unpleasantness which would unavoidably follow. This, of course, would make it unnecessary that the educator himself should become cognizant of the transgression. But this is something which has been achieved, ages ago, by traditional education, with its religious overtones: "God watches you in all you do." Such was the final argument. For indeed, if a religiously inclined child transgresses a commandment, then his pleasurable but blamable action results automatically in guilty feelings, so that here again, as in the first phase, pleasure is gained only at the cost of unavoidable discomfort. It is therefore understandable that those educators who succeed in awakening in their charges in early childhood such feelings of guilt as are connected with the pleasurable transgression of existing rules also succeed in causing the pleasure gain to be followed immediately by unpleasure. The formation in the child of such a conscious sense of guilt does not per se mean that the child's normal development is being endangered. It is only the immoderate exaggeration of this sense of guilt, and the child's exaggerated reaction to his guilty feelings, or his own repression of these feelings, that may lead to those perils which have been so clearly disclosed in the study of the neuroses.

Most parents regard their child as educable when they experience little or no resistance on his part against the efforts directed at making him accept their own scale of values. This means, in actual educational practice, that the parents are quite satisfied when they can bring up the child without excessive trouble and vexation. The child's development is then described as "normal"; he himself is said to be "normal." Otherwise he becomes "nearly uneducable, asocial, abnormal." Even when the distressed parents call upon the child guidance counselor for help, they usually do not demand more than that the child be rendered as pliant as possible. They are quite contented if through the efforts of the youth welfare worker, their child ceases to give cause for additional complaints. In most cases, it is the parents' emotional reaction to the child's attitudes that gives us a key to the child's behavior. These parents fail to grasp the true character of their children; nor can they understand the reasons for the difficulties encountered in bringing them up.

The educability of the child rests first of all upon his

physical and psychic insufficiencies. His bodily wants, his weakness, his lack of independence, his inability to provide for himself in terms of his daily bread—all this leads to his material dependence upon the grownups; while his need for affection and his incapacity to assert his own will in the face of the stronger will of the adults create in him an emotional dependence. This twofold dependence determines the position of the child, which, if stated in the child's own terms, would be described approximately as follows: "The grownup might abandon me, and thus deprive me of the love object I need; but he is also physically stronger, and could do to me whatever he pleased!" The fear of losing the adult's affection, which is the "love premium" the child so badly needs, and the anxiety caused by potential bodily dangers (castration anxiety) rob the young person of any alternatives and place him in a position of actual compulsion: he is compelled to recognize his own dependency upon the grownup, and he must therefore allow himself to be educated. This compulsive situation is the more effective—and correspondingly, the state of educability is reached the sooner—the more the child stands in need of affection. Conversely, the compulsion is weaker, and the educability is lessened, in proportion to a child's independence of the outer world in respect to his emotional relationships. To put it more briefly: the educability of the child is based upon fear of a possible withdrawal of love as well as upon castration anxiety. It would seem, therefore, that education is impossible without the emotion of fear. From this point of view, narcissism in a child is certainly an obstacle to education: the child is the less educable the more he shows independence from the adults in his own love relations—that is, in a given case, the more he is inclined to narcissism. In the later retraining of delinquent youth, especially in the rehabilitation of young swindlers, our experience leads us toward precisely the opposite conclusions. Indeed, in such cases, the relationship of the youths to their tutor stems not from object libido, but is based on narcissism.

The child's affective relationship to the educator varies

from one individual to another. But experience teaches us that education is most effective within certain limits of variation in emotional relations. There ought to be a minimum of affection, but there is also a maximum which should not be overstretched. As a love relationship dissolves, a withdrawal of affection follows until the permissible minimum is reached or falls below this minimum. And then, the libido is used up for narcissistic purposes. The tutor becomes an enemy, the latent aggressiveness comes to the fore in the child, and he can no longer be educated by the person or persons in question—at least as long as this relationship continues. Conversely, if the love relationship is intensified, reaching beyond the permissible upper limit, then the youngster becomes so sure of his tutor's, or parent's, affection—as in the case of the only child, for example—that he has no fear of withdrawal of love, whatever his own bad behavior. The anxiety situation no longer exists, and the child enjoys a twofold pleasure gain: from the primitive satisfaction of his instinctual impulses, and from the affection of his parents. This is a situation wherein the child becomes uneducable.

The means of education, i.e., reward and punishment, when considered in the context of the child's emotional relations to his educator, carry with them the following twofold warning: too much severity, the use of threats of punishment and of excessive actual punishment undermine the minimum requirements of emotional relationship on the side of the pupil; whereas too much laxity, too much mildness and kindness, may step beyond the permissible maximum. Education is possible with the help of either or both these educational means, upon condition that the emotional attachment is allowed to remain intact. Provisionally we may state the following: the decisive factor is not the kind but the amount of educational means that are being used.

As to the "economy" in education: the energies being transformed through upbringing should be used up as completely as possible for the needs of the child's inner development in the direction of the educational goal. This allows a new approach to the question of reward and punishment. If, in order to bolster up the pedagogical treatment (i.e., the prohibitions which are designed to restrain the instincts), the educator makes use of the threat of punishment, he runs the risk of inducing the pupil to use up a part of those energies which are so vitally needed for inner development, and which are now transformed into aggressiveness directed against the educator himself. Such a pedagogic method would be uneconomical in proportion to the amount of aggressive tendencies that are being diverted from the child's available energies. On the other hand, if education is brought about through mildness and kindness, there is no room for aggressiveness. The entire energy is available for the work at hand, the pedagogic work of inner transformation. Thus, education through mildness and kindness is more economical than the method which relies on threats of punishment.

Let us assume that a child is being educated only by means of mildness and kindness. He then does not experience any tendency toward aggression against the educator; and in later life, he will remain incapable of aggressive behavior. In terms of everyday practice: a person so educated will not be able to use his elbows, to push himself through the crowd. He cannot, by his own efforts, procure his own share of life's worldly, material goods. He is destined to live in dissatisfaction. But there exists indeed a way to prevent such a fate: in the process of educating a person of this kind, one may devaluate the material goods altogether, and direct the mind's interests entirely toward the ideal values, primarily the values of an afterlife. The inclination toward such a development is already laid down in his very lack of aggressiveness. On the other hand, should a child be brought up exclusively by means of threats and punishment, there follows a full development of aggressive behavior. For a person thus educated, the exclusive aim in life would be the attainment of objectives resting entirely on the material level.

If these considerations happen to be right, then there is no freedom of choice for the educator: his choice is determined by the educational goal which he must reach.

Before answering the question: "Should one prefer reward or punishment as an educational means?" we must ask yet another question. "What is the *Weltanschauung,* the ideology, in which the child is to be brought up?" An educational aim which is tinged with idealism requires as a matter of course mildness and kindness, whereas a goal resting entirely upon material values should be reached with the help of punishment. In stating these things, we are describing only one of the several factors which (according to pedagogical theory) may determine the choice of the means of education. As to the reasons that lead in practice to a mixture of the two methods, this is something which we have already discussed previously. There are cases, wherein the educational means, "reward" and "punishment," fail to work effectively: not because of a lack of proper emotional attachment, but because of particular circumstances inherent in the given case; circumstances which work against the normal effect of education or even reverse it, and produce results contrary to the one expected. In such cases, no solution at all will be found within the bounds of the dilemma of reward and punishment.

Let us illustrate this point with two examples.

A little girl, not yet six years old, has begun running away from home in the last few months. She disappears for hours at a time and is brought back home either by neighbors or by the police. The running away started a few weeks after the parents had moved into a new apartment building. Her mother explains that the child, usually quite talkative, becomes stubborn and secretive whenever she is asked to explain the reasons for her escapades. Alarmed at the growing frequency of these misdemeanors, the mother decides to visit a child guidance clinic, and brings her little girl with her. After an interview with the woman which yields no essential data that could help to clear up the case, the counselor decides to have a talk with the girl alone. The child is called in: she is a pretty, strongly built little girl, developed well beyond her age, with clever eyes and a joyful expression. She wears on her head a conspicuous dark-red knitted cap. The following conversation ensues:

"Who gave you this cap?"

"Mother."

"Do you have other caps?"

"Yes, I have a blue one, and a white one."

"Which one do you like best?"

"The red one."

"Do you like things which are red?"

"Oh yes!"

"Do you have other red things at home?"

"Certainly, we have red roses in the garden, and red carnations."

"Do you spend much time in the garden?"

"Yes. . . ."

"What do you do there?"

"I play."

"What do you play?"

"I play with my dolls."

"How many dolls have you got?"

"Three."

"What do you call them?"

"Their names are: Hansi, Fritzi, and Toni."

"Which is the smallest?"

"Toni."

"And which the tallest?"

"The girl doll, Fritzi."

"Whom do you like best?"

"Fritzi."

"And who, then, behaves worst?"

"Fritzi, of course."

"But what do you do to her when she misbehaves?"

"I beat her soundly."

"For what?"

"For running away all the time."

"And why does she run away?"

"Because she is so bored. . . ."

The little girl has clearly stated her own situation. The child guidance worker advises her mother to provide her with playmates. The woman follows this advice, and after intervals of one week, one month, three months, and half a year, she reports back to the clinic that her daughter is no longer trying to escape from home.

The child was obviously living in an unpleasant situation which she tried to avoid by running away. When such escapades are interpreted as bad behavior—as indeed they usually are—and when the "guilty" child is punished accordingly, then his feeling of unpleasure is heightened and no change of attitude takes place. If one wishes to hold a child to his own home, the home must be more attractive to the child than the world away from home.

The remarkable conclusion, in this case, would be that a child must sometimes be rewarded for his bad behavior. (The little girl was given playmates because she had been running away from home!) Such remarkable situations occur more often than most parents would wish to admit. The proper use of educational means requires consideration of the pros and cons.

Another example: A seven-year-old boy, who had been behaving well both in school and at home, begins to misbehave. His mother is at a loss what to do next, for the boy's conduct is growing worse and worse. So she seeks the advice of his schoolteacher. The teacher happens to be a modern-minded pedagogue, and he persuades the woman to ignore her son's misbehavior: she should, now as before, bestow on the boy all her love and gentle treatment. Thereupon, the behavior of the child, instead of improving, becomes more and more unbearable. His father loses patience, decides to protect himself against the "silly humanitarianism" of modern pedagogy, and wants to try out the old-fashioned method of a sound thrashing. The mother, even though she is by now inclined to agree with her husband's views, nevertheless goes to the school once more. The teacher advises again to continue the prescribed treatment of mildness and kindness, to which the youngster must sooner or later respond favorably. After that, the boy's bad behavior takes yet another turn for the worse; his father finally takes charge, and administers the long-overdue thrashing. Thereupon—lo and behold!—the bad behavior disappears abruptly. The father is very proud of himself, because his homespun pedagogy has proved better than the teacher's up-to-date methods. Yet barely a week passes by and the picture starts changing again: the boy's behavior grows worse once more, until, after another week, it has sunk to the same low level as previously. So the father again takes to the rod in a further attempt at straightening out the situation; the child's behavior improves as suddenly as before, only to deteriorate within approximately the same short span of time. This is followed, all over again, by another dose of mild and kind treatment, which proves quite as futile as the earlier doses. At this stage, the mother finally goes to the guidance clinic, where the following facts are established.

One of Franz's schoolmates had received a penknife as a birthday gift. He brought it to school and showed it to Franz, who longed to have a knife of his own. So he borrows the penknife and puts it in his pocket. Shortly thereafter, he has to go to the toilet. But Franz is hardly out of the classroom when the other boy, the rightful owner, notices the absence of his treasured property. He has meanwhile forgotten that he had lent it to Franz; and so he reports to the teacher: "Somebody has stolen my penknife!" Thereupon the teacher inquires from each boy in the class whether he has seen the object in question. At this precise moment, Franz walks back into the classroom. He hears about the "stolen" knife, but cannot admit that it is in his possession, because somehow he feels that this might be tantamount to an admission of theft. He says nothing, and sits down at his desk. But now he really feels unwell; he again must go to the washroom; and there he throws the penknife into the toilet, flushing it away for good measure, so that nobody should ever find it and brand him as a thief. Shortly afterwards, there appear the first symptoms of bad behavior in this boy.

His psychic situation may be understood approximately as follows: by throwing away the penknife, he burdened himself with a feeling of guilt, which he dares not express in words, but which nevertheless oppresses him heavily. His actions therefore acquire the character of a confession. Indeed, in every one of his acts of misbehavior there is the following admission on his part: "I am not the nice boy you believe me to be." In such instances, it is only through careful observation that an educator may recognize the psychic situation in which a child finds himself. The educator must be able to perceive clearly the presence of unconscious processes which are active in the child's psyche. The child himself does not perceive them as such, but they emerge nevertheless in the shape of actions which acquire the value of a confession.

When the youngster was being treated by methods of mildness and kindness, such treatment meant to him simply that his confession was not being understood. Parents and teachers did not change their attitudes, and thus they compelled him to go from bad to worse. This process went on until the father lost patience and started applying corporal punishment. The punishment gave the boy satisfaction, for it corresponded to his own guilty feelings, it provided him with a kind of inner liberation, and consequently the child started to behave well, suddenly, immediately after the corporal punishment. Yet this good behavior could not last for long.

A permanent improvement in the boy's behavior, with the help of such methods, would be possible only if the corporal punishment could remove the sense of guilt once and for all, but obviously this is not the case. The remedy is merely a temporary palliative.

If we consider this not as an isolated case, but recognize it as typical, then we may—with all due caution—attempt to formulate a conclusion. Every child who entertains a guilty feeling due to some secret sin, which remains unknown to the grownups, is also seeking punishment in order to satisfy this sense of guilt (unconscious need of punishment). With the decrease of the guilty feeling there is also a lessening of unpleasure—a phenomenon which is of course not at all in line with the concept of "punishment" properly so called. Thus punishment has in such cases a somewhat paradoxical effect. Instead of increasing the unpleasure, it actually provides a pleasure gain—just as if it were a reward, and not a punishment.

Yet such punishment does not liberate the child from the burden of his secret sin; a liberation could result only from outright confession. (In many instances, reparation for damages caused would also fall within this category.) Therefore, the sense of guilt cannot disappear but may be alleviated only temporarily, though during the period of such alleviation the child will behave outwardly better than he did before.

Similarly, the effects of reward may also become paradoxical, inasmuch as they cause a sharpening of the sense of guilt, and therefore an added unpleasure—such as would otherwise appear only in the case of punishment. Sometimes there occurs a temporary improvement in behavior. ("I cannot be as bad as all that if people like me so much. . . .") This improvement, however, cannot last.

In cases of well-defined masochism one observes similar effects of reward and of punishment. Whenever the educator, or the child guidance worker, happens to be aware of the functioning of these psychological mechanisms, he may look for other means than reward and punishment. He may seek several interviews, in order to trace the factual situation to its real roots, after which he may try to guide the child toward confession and reparation of damages caused, thus removing the sense of guilt, and thereby making him more accessible to training.

The cause of the guilty feelings often lies in the fairly remote past, of which no memories are left in the child's consciousness. Such a cause may arise in the period of the oedipal situation, and it often finds expression in the child's

masturbation. In these cases, mere interviews will not suffice,
and the child must be submitted to psychoanalytic treatment
in order to reveal the hidden facts in which the difficulties
happen to be rooted.

In these instances, therefore, the method of psychoanalysis
must be considered an auxiliary means of attaining the educational goal, quite on a par with the more conventional
means, which are reward and punishment.

# V

## On the Technique of Child Guidance:

## The Process of Transference

*Respectfully dedicated to
Professor Freud, on the
occasion of his 80th
birthday.*

### THE CHILD GUIDANCE WORKER AND THE PARENTS

In the performance of his tasks, the child guidance worker has no means of coercion at his disposal. As to the parents, he can do no more than make good use of the relationship he is able to establish. In this respect, his professional situation does not differ very much from that of any person whose professional success depends upon his ability to make people pliant by the power of persuasion.

For instance, a man goes to a department store to purchase, let us say, a collar button. After some time, he emerges laden with packages, and he finds himself also the proud

"Zur Technik der Erziehungsberatung: Die Übertragung." *Zeitschrift für psychoanalytische Pädagogik*, 10:5-74, 1936.

*Editor's Note:* The present essay, revised and enlarged for the *Zeitschrift für psychoanalytische Pädagogik,* has as subject a theme which the author had treated in a lecture delivered on February 29, 1936 to the Working Group for Psychoanalysis in Prague, Czechoslovakia.

possessor of a car. But he still has no collar button! What happened? The salesman has gained such an influence over his customer that the man buys whatever he is told to buy.

Another example: A young girl needed a green knitted pullover, and was inconsolable when she actually brought home an evening gown, a yellow one, which she did not need at all.

Or again: A society woman always comes back from her shopping with things for which she has no use. These repeated failures to buy what she really wants make her moody; and in order to dispel her bad mood she resorts to the following specious argument: it is worth while to have a wide selection of possible gifts for one's many acquaintances.

Yet another case: Coming home from the office one day, a husband finds his wife in a state of tearful despair. She was alone in the apartment when a salesman, selling vacuum cleaners, walked in and tried to talk her into letting him demonstrate his product. Since they already had a quite satisfactory vacuum cleaner, she absolutely refused to look at another one. Nonetheless, quite against her will, ten minutes later she had signed an order blank for a new vacuum cleaner.

What a salesman may achieve through high-pressure talks can also be accomplished—whatever his personality—by anyone holding an official position, or performing a public function, or exercising any other kind of recognized authority. When we come in contact, even in trivial matters, with officialdom or with the police, even as mere witnesses, we do not behave freely and are usually affected by a feeling of constraint which on the spot seems inexplicable to ourselves. It is only later that we become conscious of how awkwardly we have behaved, or how poorly we have carried on our affairs.

This attitude of constraint needs no particular elucidation in cases when one faces the representatives of external authority, such as police officers, or judges. But when the person who constrains us lacks this kind of authority, then our attitude of submissiveness becomes something of a mystery.

Salesmen and agents pursue a definite goal: to dispose of their goods, irrespective of the needs of their customers. In the case of the man with the collar button, or the young girl, or the society woman, or the housewife, the customer has to be made tractable even before the goods are offered to him. Indeed, things have to be so arranged that without his realizing it, or being able to oppose it, he reaches a state where he surrenders to someone's will. Of course such enforced dependence is not possible with everyone; and therefore skillful salesmen handle customers in different ways. But in the long run, they manage it usually in such a way that the buyer yields. In the examples given above, the salesman plays the part of a superior adult, while the customers behave like helpless children.

We are familiar with this sort of dependence. Each of us knows it well, for he himself has repeatedly experienced it during his own childhood. The grownups (father, mother, teacher) want something and demand it, and the child obeys without reflecting on the appropriateness of the command. Apparently, the child takes it for granted that the grownup knows best. The customer's experience, in his relation with the salesman, is not really a novel experience.

The woman who signed the order for the vacuum cleaner has met an authoritative father figure whose wishes and commands she simply *must* obey, even though her own desires run in a different direction. As to the man who set out to buy a collar button, and the girl with the yellow silk evening dress, they have encountered an even more irresistible person, the tempter who, invested with the authority of the grownup, helps them rebel against the repression of their own frustrated longings.

What are the psychic processes which contribute to such occurrences? During the time of a purchase, the salesman becomes the object of the customer's ego; whereas the id senses the influence of the libido. Something in the personality of the salesman reanimates memory traces to such an extent that the id is stimulated to duplicate in present reality those cathectic relations which actually pertain to early infantile experiences with paternal authority. The object "salesman" then becomes cathected by libido, in a manner which though not yet clear, certainly pertains to the perceptual consciousness. Freud calls this process a "false connection," for the libido which is properly connected with the father is now directed toward the person of a stranger. Since all this goes on without being perceived by the ego, the ego becomes deluded and accepts a stranger, namely, the salesman, as the paternal authority for the duration of the sale. The function of critical judgment is suspended, the superego is taken over from the person of the salesman, and a process which originally led to the formation of the superego itself is now made retrogressive. On the other hand, the childish dependency also determines a loss of critical judgment in the customer. Should the salesman offer wares which would satisfy some repressed cravings in the buyer (the car, the yellow silk evening dress), then the paternal authority becomes a force of irresistible temptation. The ego and the superego not only fail to antagonize each other, but come to easy terms, and the ego freely experiences those pleasures which are associated with a permissible gratification of instincts.

This type of relationship is known to us elsewhere; we encounter it as "transference" during successful psychoanalytic treatment. In the process of transference, infantile experiences are reproduced, either through remembrance (as in psychoanalysis) or through repetition. And this repetition, in acts or in attitudes, is called "acting out."

What can we learn from those "shopping situations" described above?

Under the pressure of transference, action can be forced into specific channels and conveniently used for the attainment of definite purposes.

THE CHILD GUIDANCE WORKER AS A LIBIDINAL OBJECT

This set of psychic facts, if rightly interpreted and made use of at the appropriate moment, offers the counselor at the child guidance clinic certain advantages in his work that should not be underestimated. Our task now is to present more information on this subject.

It will be well first to make a few general remarks about the nature of child guidance. The name "child guidance clinic" is not entirely appropriate for describing the function of such clinics, as in most instances mere "guidance" does not prove sufficient. Help in child rearing has to be extended. As a rule, parents bring their children to the clinic only when the usual means of rearing, reward and punishment, have become ineffectual, and when the emotional disturbance of the child is fast approaching a crisis, or has reached a state of constantly recurring conflict. The child guidance clinic is scarcely thought of as a prophylactic institution.

In practice, child guidance has to deal with emotional crises. The worker must establish the causes of the trouble, prescribe the means for its removal, or participate in the treatment. Should the emergency arise from a childhood or adolescence neurosis or psychosis, then the task of the counselor is completed when he has referred the case to a psychoanalyst. However, he will have to take upon himself most of the tasks needed for the child's recovery in the following cases: in the many and variegated forms of delinquency for which there is not yet an established symptomatology; in composite forms of delinquency and neurosis; and in all those conditions which cannot be sufficiently characterized because they lack well-delineated symptoms. The emergencies which are caused by social or economic insufficiencies require other efforts from the child guidance worker, but a discussion of this problem would fall outside the scope of this paper.

Among the various groups and cells of which society is composed, the family represents a peculiar elementary reality, determined by its own libidinal structure. The mutually libidinal relations between the various members of the family, the "intrafamilial libido constellation," is much more important in determining the child's future than those coexisting and subsequent libidinal relations they may have with the external milieu. A thoroughgoing exploration of the causes of delinquency will accomplish nothing if the clinic staff regards the child as a self-contained "defective object" and does not take into account the unique place the child has in the libidinal structure of his family. Only those workers who grasp all the effects of these reciprocal relationships will discover the subterranean paths which lead to delinquency.

For example, the battle which rages between child and parents is clearly visible in all cases of waywardness. Indeed, this struggle is too often taken for granted as a self-evident and necessary concomitant, and therefore is not regarded as something that might illuminate the causes of delinquency. In this way one fails to take advantage of a valuable approach to the problem.

In the course of the conflict between child and parents, the adults hold the upper hand for a long time. Eventually the parental weapons grow more and more blunted, and when the parents finally come to the child guidance clinic, they are already on the defensive. Indeed, they now expect that we should provide them with reinforcements which have become necessary to overcome the adversary. Since they are conscious only of their desire to help the child, they would not only be astonished to hear such an explanation; in all probability they would reject it with vehemence. And withal, their behavior tells us of their wish to make the child pliant again.

There are instances in which the battle between mother and child follows a very stormy course, and where separate phases of the conflict may be clearly perceived. Observation of the mother's attitude during the clinic visits gives the impression that she overburdens the child with her affection; that she lays excessive claim to the child as her own libido object. We know that in such cases, the child's reaction sets in at an early stage. The critical point at which the basic defense mechanisms start developing either toward neurosis or toward delinquency is reached at a time when the increased defense reactions are not yet perceptible to people in the child's environment. But with the progressive development of these latent forms of waywardness, the ever-growing defense reactions begin to manifest themselves outwardly, and the struggle with the mother ensues. Without quite realizing it, the mother feels that her own stronghold is collapsing, and she does her very best to hold the fort. She takes care of the child more strenuously than ever, she devotes all her attention to him, and seems to live only for the child's sake —but all to no avail. The child reacts to everything with a completely negative attitude, incomprehensible to his mother. She does not know that actually her own behavior is being sensed correctly by the child: for in truth, her efforts are not at all directed toward the person, or the wishes, of the child, but rather toward the re-establishment, at the youngster's expense, of a now sadly disrupted intrafamilial libidinal equilibrium.

In the next phase of this conflict the maternal strivings assume a new coloring. The mother's statements confirm unequivocally that her unconscious efforts have no other aim but to claim the child for herself: "You are ungrateful, I have no one but you, and this is how you reward my love!" etc. She expects that the child will respond to this by submitting to her will, but she suffers yet another disappointment. Thus far, the child has had only an indefinite, though correct, feeling about his mother's behavior. Now her remarks confirm his feelings—albeit not at all in the sense hoped by his mother. He may now quite consciously take action against her. At this point the battle enters the stage in which the child becomes progressively stronger, while the mother loses ground, is forced on the defensive, and finally comes to seek our help. Indeed, the child has now become not only intolerably aggressive toward her, but he also shows symptoms of delinquency. The mother begs us to put her wayward child on the straight path again. We accept the child in treatment; we do what the mother consciously desires, and thereupon we often experience an incomprehensible resistance on her part against the recovery of her child. And sure enough, the treatment of the child fails in such cases unless he is removed from the home. But if we do remove the child, we learn after a short time that the mother is now developing neurotic symptoms. We begin to discover the hidden pathways which have led to the child's delinquency. The mother, in order to keep her own neurotic symptoms in abeyance, had libidinally overburdened her child. We have learned that the advice we give the parents, in the interest of the child, only increases their distress; and even when they consciously wish to follow our suggestions, they are unable to do so because of an inner, unconscious resistance. As a result, a child guidance worker can seldom appeal to the parents' judgment; instead, he must find ways and means of setting up a contact with their unconscious self.

This is not especially difficult, provided that the counselor is able to establish the right kind of relationship with the parents—in other words, a successful transference. As a result of this relation of dependency between parents and counselor, he is able to guide the behavior of the parents in such a way as to serve the purposes of the therapeutic work. A basis has been established for taking care of the emergency situation in the bringing up of the child.

It also follows that a child guidance worker may expect a quicker and easier success if he is willing at the start to give his full attention to the parents rather than to the child. This may seem startling, paradoxical, even untrue: for if it be the child whom we desire to help, is it not chiefly upon him that we should focus our interest from the very outset? And yet, experience has proved time and again that it is far easier to overcome the distress if one takes the parents as the important element and concentrates upon them in a first, preparatory stage. Cases which require direct, immediate help and thus call for a different type of intervention are infrequent. The child guidance worker should not allow his personal interest in the child to divert him from the path indicated above; on the contrary, he should devote his efforts, unhurriedly and deliberately, to the first task, which is to establish a transference relationship with the parents.

As we have noted, there is always an inner struggle in the families of delinquents; the very progress of this struggle indicates the existence of an emergency in the libidinal "household" of the parents and influences their readiness to invest somewhere their libido, which is now in a state of instability. Their description of the difficulties the child has caused them at home and in school, the aggressively impassionate or resigned mood in which they relate the woes and sorrows they have suffered at his hands—all this gives the counselor concrete indications that help him shape his own behavior. When he sees that the youngster, in his exasperated attitude of defense, has reached a point where his conduct is unbearable, it becomes easier for the worker to identify himself, if only for a brief moment, with the parents, thus giving proof to them of his own participation in their predicament. In doing so, he satisfies their unconscious need for a libidinal object. One cannot stress too much that the first requirement is to set aright the disturbed intrafamilial libidinal equilibrium; and that this should be effected by the counselor, who offers his own person to the parents as a proper object. The initial, preparatory stage in every case of child guidance is completed only when the child guidance worker is accepted in this role by the parents themselves.

THE ESTABLISHMENT OF LIBIDINAL RELATIONS

If the transference is to succeed, we must first of all exercise a special skill: the skill of being a good listener. This is not so easy; in fact, it is much more difficult than being a good speaker. In our work, to be a good listener does not mean simply to take in everything that is said; or to suppress one's impulse to follow up one's own divergent thoughts; or to avoid asking questions, no matter how appropriate they may be, if these questions result from one's newly awakened interest, and are likely therefore to prevent the client from following his original inclination. The process of proper listening entails that the worker accompany the verbalizations of the client with his own associations; in this way he can grasp directly the "why" that underlines what is being said as well as the connections being revealed, the emotions expressed, and certain changes in the attitudes of the speaker himself. Why is the parent saying just this particular thing? Why is this thing mentioned in a particular connection? Why is this specific emotion manifested at this point, although it does not seem to fit the context? Why does it pick up speed at some other point? And why, when a certain relationship between facts or statements is being brought to his attention, does the speaker react with a gesture of defense or acceptance, a gesture which seems to be quite out of keeping with his previous attitudes? Why? Why? . . .

Thus the counselor will be able to find the right moment, and the parents will spontaneously feel they are speaking to a person more understanding than anyone they have ever met before.

It takes parents some time to make themselves understood. We wait patiently, without prodding them, and without indicating by a wink, or by any other sign, that this or that detail is unimportant, irrelevant, or repetitious. We let them give their description in a connected or a disconnected way. They may enlarge on something if they wish; they may enter into particulars or not, as they see fit. And they may unburden themselves in any way they are able or willing. We start asking questions only when their talk ceases to flow, when they become silent, or when we observe that they are not capable of formulating their thoughts. However, these questions should arise only from our own associations which accompany their talk and therefore do not interfere with the freely flowing thoughts and emotions of the parents.

Such questions serve only to stimulate and strengthen the impulses already present. Our basic attitude to the problem requires that we refrain from any attempt to lead the conversation so that it corresponds to some pre-established scheme, or to some written form which the parent would have to fill out, or to any other prescribed order and sequence. Indeed, it is not our task to set the line for communication; this line must arise solely from the emotional state of those who now sit in front of us. In this manner we create a substitute for the method of free association (which we know from psychoanalysis), and bring about an atmosphere in which the transference may develop. It is unimportant whether in the first interview we get any considerable material of anamnesis, any data concerning the prehistory of the case. Indeed, the personal relationship which we manage to establish is of infinitely greater importance for the future course of our work.

But even before the parents sit down with us and begin to speak, there are important moments which should not be allowed to slip away without being used to good effect. Relationships which would make transference difficult or impossible might conceivably arise before the conversation gets underway. The kind of reception we accord the parents is therefore not a matter of indifference. Are we ready to turn all our attention toward them, or are we still somewhat preoccupied with the previous case; do we go out to greet them, do we receive them standing, or sitting; whether and in what manner we extend our hand to them; do we meet them with a serious or a friendly expression; and are we looking them straight in the face, or do we look past them? A slight but suggestive gesture, a barely perceptible nod, a more active or a more passive attitude just at the right moment—all these may bring into play imponderable factors of great potency.

It is difficult to establish any universally valid rules just as it is hard to state or record all the individual situations in which one might be involved. However, two comments seem to me of considerable importance. The first: we usually tend to overvalue the things we say, while underrating the necessity of listening, during our first contacts with parents and children. The other: not everything required for successful child guidance work can be acquired through mere learning. It is difficult to do well in this sort of work without a good measure of talent for empathy, a capacity for intuitive understanding. On the other hand, should this native capacity be too strong, then the counselor will tend to develop intense identifications which may undermine the objectivity necessary for investigation. In this case, which actually happens with many women, the worker is unfit to give help because of the depth of his own sympathy. But even with a proper, well-balanced capacity for empathy, the power of successful intervention may still be weakened, if the counselor lacks the ability to reach clear-cut decisions appropriate to his aim.

THE PLANNED INFLUENCING OF DIFFERENT TYPES OF PARENTS

*"Acting Out" Based on the Transference of Id Impulses*

Let us now turn to the mother who strives to fend off the symptoms of her own neurosis, and in doing so causes her child to become delinquent. If we behave in the manner indicated above, then the mere fact of being able to vent her emotions in unrestrained expression will lead her to form a libidinal attachment to us. If we show understanding, if the mother perceives that we are interested in her difficulties and have a desire to share her problem, if we do not become impatient and are entirely at her disposal during the period of our interview, then there must inevitably follow a transference through the mechanism of "false connection." The woman is now in a position similar to that of the customer in respect to the salesman. In fact, her attachment to the worker will probably be much stronger, and certainly more enduring.

From the mother's account we shall presumably have

learned a great deal about the acute conflict she faces, about conditions within the family, about the psychic situation of the child, and about the kind of upbringing she experienced in her childhood (for, without her noticing it, we have steered the conversation in that direction also). Meanwhile, we have been able to select the best opening for our first intervention. Indeed, we know now what it is the mother's behavior which particularly annoys the child and provokes in him the strongest defensive reactions. Our intervention will therefore aim at influencing the mother to control her emotions. This will being about a change in the attitude of the child, and lead toward a general lessening of tensions at home.

However, neither mere hints nor more sweeping suggestions are enough to produce the intended changes in the mother's behavior. Direct instruction is needed, and we must give it in the form of commands: clearly understandable directions, unequivocal as to content, presented in such a precise manner that no room is left for doubts, and performance must follow. Thus, under the pressure of transference, the mother is compelled to act out her part not only in keeping with our wishes, but under our guidance.

The worker must bear in mind that in no case should his orders shake or endanger the transference. This he may prevent by the manner in which he proceeds. The counselor must insinuate himself unnoticed into the mother's superego, in such a way that his commands are experienced not as something alien, but as her own wish, arising from her own superego. There are exceptions, of course: in cases where from the first interview, the worker is accepted as a paternal authority, which cannot be contradicted. He then proceeds to make demands from this position of authority.

However, if we have failed to take the proper attitude, for instance, if we have overestimated the strength of the transference, we soon observe our error in the way the mother behaves at the clinic, or still more distinctly, in her own home. She is critical of us, she either does not consider our instructions at all, or regards them only as a piece of advice to be followed or disregarded at will; she goes on having emotional outbursts, she either fails to carry out our prescription, or carries it out in an incomplete or incorrect manner.

On the other hand, if the mother acts out her part correctly at home, then the preparatory stage of the treatment may be considered complete, and the child moves now into the foreground.

At this point several questions must arise: How long will the mother be able to endure the bad behavior of her child without relapsing herself? How long will we keep the mother dependent upon us? And how will we undo the network of transference, so as to reinstate the mother to her personal freedom of action?

Concerning the first question: once the mother starts "acting out" under our influence, we do not leave her to her own devices; we arrange to see her a second time, only a few days later, and at brief regular intervals thereafter, depending on the intensity of the transference nexus. By that means, and by means of our subsequent behavior (which does not differ significantly from our conduct during the first interview), we exclude the possibility of a change in her relationship to us: any slackening of the transference is prevented, the mother's resistance to her own emotional outbursts is strengthened, and, furthermore, conditions are created which enable her better to endure her child, should his behavior get worse. Indeed, we must prepare the mother to face this eventuality. For the child will not always experience the strengthening of the mother's libidinal relationship to us, with an easing of his own burden, as something necessarily pleasant and beneficent. He may even grow suspicious, or his reactions may already have developed into such a solid structure that the pressures which his mother used to exercise upon him have now become indispensable to his equilibrium. In either case, his provocations against his mother are likely to increase and to manifest themselves in progressively intolerable behavior.

As long as the mother's transference to our person remains

unwavering, she will be able to endure her child's bad temper, his expressions of waywardness, and his increasing provocations, without relapsing into her former errors.

As to the other questions, they would readily answer themselves if only it were possible to submit the mother herself to a timely psychoanalysis. Since this may be done only in rare instances, it becomes important to answer these questions too.

How long do we keep the mother dependent upon us? After the preliminary stage there follows a second phase, during which the child comes into the foreground and a remedy is sought for his emotional disturbance. During this period we do not as a rule allow any change to occur in the mother's relationship to us, even though there are certain exceptionally favorable cases where a slackening in the relationship may be permitted. But in most instances, while we note carefully any tendency which might render the relationship negative or cause the transference to dissipate, we take steps in good time to prevent this from taking place. Not until the crisis is so far resolved that no difficulties remain except those which are normal in the training of any child, do we conclude this portion of our work, and with it the entire second phase.

The duration of the mother's transference relationship to us is determined by the duration of the family crisis.

The opening of the third phase, in which the liberation of the mother occurs, is not definable with any degree of precision: in fact, the transition is so gradual that the two phases cannot be clearly separated. Theoretically, the last phase of the work is completed when the mother has become entirely independent of the counselor; this means ideally that she has achieved full freedom to deal with her child. But this ideal situation is seldom attained all at once. Residues of the former transference often persist for lengthy periods. However, experience has shown us that far from harming either the mother or the child, such residual elements of transference may become useful again, should any difficulties reappear within the family; and therefore we leave it to the action of time alone to erase these lingering traces of transference. Moreover, they often work themselves out favorably in the upbringing of other children in the family. It will sometimes happen that a mother will work against the recovery of her child merely out of an unconscious desire to come to see us again and again. But it is easy to recognize this tendency and to render it harmless.

The procedure in the third phase of the work differs substantially from that of the first and second. In the first two periods, we did not rely much on the intellectual ego of the mother; our efforts were focused on her emotional ego; the reason being that she was still unable at that time to master her own emotions, either by herself or with the help of such insights as we may have acquired. We demanded repeatedly that she should control the expression of her feelings through reliance on her relationship with us; in so doing we really were applying our own personality to the task of steadying the emotional balance within the family.

Now in the third phase this situation undergoes a change. No longer do we appear only in the role of a benign authority who merely appreciates and praises. We start cautiously to criticize, nor do we hesitate any longer to blame an action or attitude brought to our attention. In fact, we start behaving gradually in such a way that we incite the mother to contradict us. Thus we reawaken in her that critical faculty which had been dormant.

Once this has been successfully accomplished, we try further to enliven the mother's critical ego by criticizing her in a manner which grows more and more impersonal and matter of fact, and by encouraging an exchange of ideas into which we enter readily and at length.

The next step is the strengthening of the mother's ability to judge by herself. We get her to produce her own suggestions, with which we agree, or which we reject after a detailed explanation. Thus we progressively withdraw to the position of a mere adviser.

Our further efforts are now aimed at a severance of the bond which ties her to our judgment and to our person, as well as the complete reconstruction of her superego. The mother carries out measures we have suggested on her own responsibility or even plans she herself has submitted. We give recognition to each independent achievement, and we find out together the possible causes of any failure.

Finally, the mother stands by our side as an equal, and at this point we dare engage in a common search for those relationships which may explain the behavior and waywardness of the youngster. This is the time when she can rid herself of her previous unrealistic overestimation of our person— an overestimation due solely to the phenomenon of transference, which is now replaced by a normal acceptance of the counselor.

Thus, as a result of our deliberate planning, the mother has at last recovered her superego, and is now able to withdraw that libido which up to this point had been invested in us.

A part of the libido which has thus been liberated returns once again to the child. However, as a result of our guidance, the new libidinal change is used in a quite different way: the mother has by now learned a great deal about the external circumstances and inner difficulties which plague her child; she understands something about his strivings, wishes, and needs; and therefore she is able at last to apply a considerable amount of libido to the exacting task of rearing the child, to estimate correctly the various psychic conditions wherein her child may find himself, which are to be met by granting or withholding the proper amounts of libido. As to the "surplus" part of the mother's libido (if there is any), it should by this time already be invested in some other sphere of interest, unconnected with the child.

A similar problem is the case of the frustrated woman who seeks a substitute gratification through some abnormal interest in the sexual manifestations of her child. Of course she is quite unaware of this, and only believes herself to be more attentive than other mothers are and to be rearing her child especially well. Such women live in a state of constant tension and anxiety about their child's physical and moral well-being. In extreme cases, they seem to be possessed by an intense and almost compulsive need to find out suggestive information: they look for any hint of sexual impulses or forbidden practices on the part of the child; indeed, masturbation and all that pertains to it are usually in the center of their search. As a result, we might well anticipate that the child's sexuality will be aroused early and will soon be led into aberrant paths. These women torture themselves for a long time in secret observation of the child, without really interfering with his actions. If the proper guidance is provided early enough, there is seldom any serious harm done to the child.

In a case of this sort, we are not necessarily dealing with an overly libidinized child, and with a crisis in his upbringing. But it is obvious that the child is in grave danger, and that it is only a matter of a short time before he finds himself in a predicament.

Our behavior toward this type of woman differs in no respect from that described above. The course of the introductory phase is the same, with only one difference: from the outset, our critical attention is able to follow the fluctuating emotions with which the mother denounces her "rotten" child. In that way we avoid an error that could be disastrous. We do not always have neurotic parents who exaggerate beyond all measure the harmless expressions of a child's sexuality, and then come to us for help. There are also nonneurotic parents who appear with accounts of observations about the abnormal sexual development of their child. As to a parent who struggles against his or her own repressed sexual desires, this is easy to note if only we are alert. A special readiness for transference in such instances shortens the introductory work considerably.

In the second phase, our task consists in diverting the sexual interest of the mother away from her child. By means of our questions, we approach the situation in such a way that she is never quite conscious of what we are doing. We do not wish to arouse any opposition, for otherwise we would have to concentrate on that. Our questions consist of an indirect inquiry into the mother's feelings at the time when her observations were made. This technique alerts the ego, without expressly stating in words what it is that should attract its attention. Indeed, in the absence of any verbal representations, the ego cannot take care of the newly awakened tension state. But we can hope to reach a successful outcome only if we avoid provoking a critical situation, and this is what we are trying to do when we divert the mother's sexual interests from her observations. When the woman becomes alerted, she is capable of showing some understanding for the other needs of the child, and she no longer regards the normal expressions of his sexuality with the same aversion as before, but can accept them as rather harmless. Consequently, there is no longer any danger of the mother's developing an excessive libidinal interest in her child.

It is appropriate at this point to mention a case I published elsewhere (1932), that of a mother who was led astray by her own unconscious wish fantasies, until she accused her daughter of a manifest homosexual relationship with the girl's teacher. Two typical cases of a similar kind may be quoted here, in order to illustrate the way in which the adult's interest is directed toward the awakening sexual life of the child.

In a certain proletarian environment, there were adults who lived in complete sexual freedom. Because of the crowded housing conditions, ten or more persons commonly slept together in a single room. Mother and father would sleep of course in one bed, so would the grown-up brothers and sisters, together with their boy and girl friends. The most intimate intercourse would take place in the presence of the children, sometimes without any restraint, though often with some attempt at concealment; but even then, there would be little effort required on the part of the child to observe what was taking place. However, the striking thing was the attitude of the *adults* toward the children. The grownups showed a unanimously inquisitive concern about the children's masturbation; for in these families, the children are strictly forbidden to masturbate.

It is one of the most difficult problems in child guidance work, and one that often baffles every effort, to try to make a child's sexual behavior comprehensible to an absolutely indignant mother, in terms of the youngster's environment. We regularly get the following reply: "Just what does the little wretch think he is doing!" This reaction would perhaps be understandable if the mother held the rather conventional opinion that the child might injure himself, and if she were motivated by such fears. Yet actually, the dominant feeling is one of indignation at the child for claiming a right which belongs only to adults.

Time and again, we come across cases of foster mothers who have been entrusted by various social or municipal agencies with the care of children of preparatory school age. They describe in the most emotional manner what they have observed concerning the masturbation of the foster children. These mothers are by no means lacking in experience about the ways and mentality of the child; in fact, they may have three or four children of their own, one of whom might be in the same age group as the foster child. If it happens, even once, that the child has shocked his foster mother by sexual behavior, he then comes under almost unceasing observation, in which every grown member of the family takes part. The child's masturbation becomes the center of conversation. Not only are friends and neighbors consulted, but also the doctor at the welfare agency, the social worker, the head counselor, and all other officials: they are informed about what has been discovered, and every conceivable technique is enlisted in this battle against masturbation. One wonders why more barbaric devices are not employed in such circumstances and why it does not come to actual mistreatment of the child. Apparently, the pent-up emotions expend themselves in keeping the culprit under observation, in discussing his case, and in consulting the authorities about it all. In one respect, all these families are in agreement: their *own* children never behaved in this way. Every attempt to reason with such people remains fruitless. A successful outcome can be achieved only by establishing a transference relationship.

The examples given above still require a good deal of theoretical clarification of the behavior of the adults. When we know more about it, we will be able to achieve transference with greater certainty, because this relationship will then be planned in advance. But at present, since we must rely merely on our own intuitive grasp of each situation, nothing can be suggested as to the proper technique to employ.

The repressed wish fantasies of the adults do not always find their satisfaction in an intensive observation of a child's primitive sexual behavior. The pathogenic conflicts break out in other areas, if these happen to offer a more favorable outlet. In such cases, the child's sexual life becomes unimportant to his parents; indeed, they do not even seem to notice its existence. But every act which complements some parental defect assumes exaggerated importance; it draws to itself the entire interest of the parents, it appears to them as something quite unusual, and they react to it by surrounding the child with excessive concern. These are the circumstances in which the alleged cases of "hysterical vomiting," of "obsessional neurosis," and of "juvenile delinquency' are brought to the attention of the child guidance clinic. Yet in reality, a frail child will often have an upset stomach; or a youngster will be more orderly, more fussy than usual, perhaps commendably so, or a little more lively and less well behaved than other children. We hear from the mouth of the parents circumstantial, wordy accounts about awful scenes at home, which did really happen, as we may learn after checking the facts. But the parents do not notice that such scenes are secondary phenomena arising from their own irrational behavior. Nor do they realize how they themselves are tormenting the child, whose natural defense reactions they entirely misunderstand. When we get to see such children, the situation, as a rule, has not yet reached a state of emergency; or, to put it differently, the situation is similar to that of the children who are brought to us because of their "sexual depravity." In both categories, however, the child must be considered to be in grave danger.

The treatment of these cases must proceed according to the scheme we have already presented above; except for the proviso that the child guidance worker must be especially alert in noticing immediately any distortions in the parent's report. Otherwise the counselor is likely to be led astray, because the child, frightened and intimidated by his parents, will seem to bear out their account completely. The worker might thus arrive at an erroneous diagnosis and attack the problem from a false angle, which leads only to failure. Conversely, if he evaluates the parental type quickly and accurately, then he is in a position to make the proper decisions on the basis of such repressed material as is revealed by the parents' communications, which are variously charged with affects; and at last he may set in motion a transference which has been well planned in advance.

We approach the limits of what our guidance can possibly achieve when we encounter domestic situations wherein the parental neurosis takes a form which seriously injures the child, while the parents themselves show no propensity for taking any steps toward a cure of their own sickness. In my paper on "Child Guidance" (1932) I described a case of educational emergency which arose from a mother's obsessional hand washing. We were able to treat this case successfully only because it was possible to submit this woman to psychoanalysis.

In all types of family crises so far described, the preparatory phase followed an identical pattern, with such slight differences as were required to fit each individual case. This technique, however, is appropriate only in those instances where a neurotic ego structure results in a more or less passive behavior.

With other types of parents, the sort of transference induced by these methods might take a long time, but the desired relationship may be brought about quickly if our patient waiting is suddenly replaced by an active approach. The success depends essentially on the tempo of this change. The shorter the interval between the passive and the active phases, the greater is the initial surprise, and the more profound the effect.

To illustrate this point further, let us consider the behavior of a child guidance worker in a typical instance. The largest percentage of delinquent children comes from families wherein the distribution of authority between the parents is the reverse of the normal situation. The mother is the head of the family; she rules her husband and children; she decides what shall be done; she takes the domineering role as a matter of course. At the same time, she is far from noticing how oppressive she is to the members of her own household; on the contrary, she is convinced that without her the family could not get along. The father acknowledges the superior position of his wife. Unconsciously, he is quite happy with it, and allows her to lead and rule without much opposition. Consciously, he regards himself as the more reasonable member of the family, who submits patiently and mostly without grumbling, for the sake of having peace at home. As to his own occasional rebellions, he is hardly aware of them, for they collapse almost as soon as they start. He can be aroused only by exceptional provocation, but then he flares up in insensate fury and becomes brutal. These outbursts are often so violent that wife and children must either flee from home or, in some other social milieu, withdraw in terror as if he were dangerously insane.

The active woman, a latent homosexual, is confronted by a passive man who is also a latent homosexual. A man of this type experiences the activity of the woman as if it were an aggression and a castration threat; he fails to realize what it actually is: an unconscious wish to be conquered by a powerful male. He is never able to gratify this much stronger unconscious impulse of the woman, and he repeatedly disappoints her. It is likely that her greatest disillusionment comes at the time when he turns brutal, for even then, far from showing himself a strong man, he is either an uncontrolled irrational weakling or seems mentally sick. As a matter of fact, he is overwhelmed by his emotions, just like a raging infant who kicks everything around him. And even though he may strike terror in his own house, he is still quite unable to alter his position in the family.

The libidinal demands of his wife go unsatisfied, either because they are not recognized at all, or because she herself withdraws them, after becoming frightened by her husband's behavior. At this point, the woman must cast about for some other adequate object, and the child is first in line. The child is thus drawn into a chaotic state which must be organized and reach equilibrium, at his own expense. But the child cannot endure such a constant, excessive, libidinal burden without becoming injured, and so we presently get another case of juvenile delinquency at the clinic.

The usually passive attitude with which we meet parents, during out initial interviews with them, strikes a mother of this type as something familiar. Indeed, she is led astray by our deliberately planned behavior, and without the slightest hesitation she tries to treat us in exactly that way which has always so brilliantly succeeded at home. She thinks she stands on well-explored ground, where no unexpected reactions are to be anticipated. Whereupon we abruptly abandon our passive role, often in the space of a split second. In our subsequent behavior, she now experiences something entirely new, something quite unknown to her, yet something which she has been unconsciously longing for: an inflexible will in another person, against which she storms in vain.

It is obvious that the particular behavior of each counselor will depend on his own personality; but we must take it for granted that he will avoid any emotional entanglement. Experience teaches us that this sudden reversal in the behavior of the social worker creates such a tremendous shock that there ensues a particularly intensive transference.

Let us consider the psychic situation of this mother: if we deal with it according to the pattern of all the cases described, we should logically conclude that in her case also we must keep our conduct as free as possible from any reactions, so as to facilitate the establishment of a transference. Yet actually, with a woman of this type, the result would not be the one we had expected. Such a woman would get nothing of importance out of all our counseling; her experiences at our clinic would not influence her life in any decisive way; she would have only recreated the same old situation, so familiar to her from her own married life: that of a passive man, who bends without resistance under a storm of aggressive demands.

We wish to achieve something quite different. We neglect the conscious and visible libidinal attitude of the mother, for we recognize in it a mere product of defense and denial; instead, we direct our attention to the deeper unconscious layers. We set ourselves up as an opponent, and thus we fulfill her own unconscious and deeply repressed wish: the yearning for the strong man, by whom she must allow herself to be conquered.

I have reported elsewhere (1932) the case of an alcoholic father, and I have explained there what had created an unbearable situation in this family. His was a form of alcoholism we frequently encounter in such families where the distribution of power between the two parents is abnormally reversed. What we do then is to help the mother achieve a passive attitude, and to help the father express his aggressive tendencies in some socially acceptable way.

The type of help we may give to the mother can be seen in the example submitted above. As to the father, we must bring him into a different sort of relationship to us. Experience shows that such fathers always come from a family background closely similar to that one which they tend to create in their own married lives. With a husband of this type, the inner attitudes toward the wife—and often also the corresponding outward behavior—are merely the continuation of the relationship with his own mother. That he himself is unaware of this fact is usually due entirely to external differences between the two women: his wife has different features, her eyes or hair are of another color, she is unlike her mother-in-law in gestures and appearance, etc. By and large, however, in all those characteristics that are important in people who live together, the wife happens to be a precise copy of the mother. Furthermore, the position of a man of this type in respect to his father is also of decisive importance in determining his behavior within the family. As a child he repeatedly experienced that his own father was a weakling who could not assert himself against the mother. During the paternal outbreaks of rage and frenzy, he identified himself with his mother and took her side, while rejecting his father entirely. During these crises he felt it his duty to protect her from such a violent man. Thus he lacked a father object which would have helped him to develop into a normal man.

Both parents are frequently called to the child guidance clinic, but of course they are interviewed separately. A successful outcome is likely only after intensive work with both. Under pressure of the transference, the mother "acts out" her part at home in a manner suggested by the counselor: she controls her emotions far better than before, and is much more tractable. She even gives a chance to her husband, who may now put in a few words. The latter considers this acting out as a definite change, which he credits to the worker; a change that seems not only extraordinarily pleasant, but also entirely incomprehensible. Thus the counselor becomes in his eyes something like an admired father, who does not yield to his wife, and against whom she dare not rebel.

But he experiences much more than that: the purposeful intervention of the counselor, his understanding comments, his kindliness, also create an imaginary mother picture. Something of the man's childhood fantasies now becomes reality. The counselor is the great benign wizard who gathers within himself a total omnipotence, but who need not be feared, for he is in no sense sinister; rather he is to be obeyed gladly and willingly. Many cramped feelings are released, and forces within the personality which had been locked in mutually destructive struggles have now been freed for useful activities. Both parents are gradually liberated from the shackles of their previous, critical state. But for a long time thereafter, the child guidance worker still remains the supreme authority which is invoked again and again, and to which both parents willingly submit. At last, even this stage in the relationship is slowly overcome, and what remains is a great experience with deep psychological aftereffects.

## *"Empathy": The Intuitive Understanding of the Parents' Superego*

In order to establish a transference to our person, we can make use of the id, the ego, and the superego of the parents. In coping with the types of emergencies described so far, it seemed appropriate to turn preponderantly toward the id, through the mediation of the ego. In certain cases, however, we may reach our goal more readily and with greater certainty by following another way, namely, by using the ego's dependence on the superego. But a child guidance worker can enlist the ego for his own purposes only if he has a good knowledge of that social environment which encompasses the person seeking advice. If the counselor knows how the parents themselves have been brought up, how life is lived in their particular milieu, and what aims seem worth while to them, then by the same token he is also aware of their attitudes toward the suprapersonal, toward their own religious needs, and toward those ethical and moral principles which rule their conduct. Nor is he unfamiliar with that standard of values which they apply to both the ideal and the material goods of life. The more exactly the counselor is informed about the content of the parents' superego, the easier it will be for him, at the proper moment, to induce these parents to follow him willingly and with conviction. The manner in which the superego of the parents exerts its control over their ego—whether it compels brutally, or admonishes hesitatingly, or almost begs to act or to refrain from action—this is something which a trained eye and ear can perceive in the external behavior of the parents during their visits at the clinic. Indeed, it is essential that a counselor should be able and willing to grasp both the content and the form of the parents' superego; for it is upon such ability and willingness that the success of his entire task depends.

In contrast to the cases described previously, we are dealing now with situations wherein we do not want the parents to give up their own power of judgment, and act out almost automatically whatever the counselor expects. Quite the contrary: the persons of the type with which we are now concerned must themselves experience the fact that the counselor regards the demands of their superego as fully justified. Indeed, it is now up to the counselor to behave as though his own critical judgment were submerged. And therefore he can but agree with the parents' evaluation of the distress that brings them to the clinic.

For instance, a father comes to us with his only child, a thirteen-year-old boy, who has been required to repeat his grade in high school, and who shows such poor progress even in this second year that he is in danger of being dismissed from school altogether. According to the father's description, the boy could study much better if he only wanted to. But he is lazy, and shows great reluctance when compelled to do his schoolwork. He is stubborn and insolent; but when left alone, reserved and taciturn. He has no friends, no interests; and when at home, he sits idly and stares into the void.

The father makes a strikingly good impression. Although merely an unskilled worker, he is well dressed for his circumstances, speaks a cultured language, and seems far better

educated than one would expect. Indeed, he is well read and
unusually well informed about current issues. He leads a
modest, economically very restricted, but well-ordered life.
His only interest lies in his son. He lives exclusively for this
boy, he wants to build a good future for him and considers
a high school education as the most reliable basis for the
future. In fact, this father has renounced every personal pleasure: he has even given up smoking to provide more money
for school. And now the boy disappoints him! The father is
now thoroughly upset that all his self-denials and exertions
have remained fruitless. It makes him especially bitter to
think that his child, who does not realize his sacrifices, has
not only withdrawn into himself, but has actually come to
hate his father.

During our first interview with this man, even before we
got to know the son, the situation became much clearer since
we managed the conversation in such a way as to make the
father talk about himself and about his childhood. He
comes from a family of manual workers, where hunger was a
frequent experience, but where happiness was far from unknown. The mother had a sunny nature; the father was a
kind man who dearly loved his wife and children, especially
his elder son—our present client. In elementary school, he
was always first in his grade. He had no greater ambition
than to go to high school, but just before he was to enter
junior high, his father died, and the entire family found itself
in dire need. He had to give up all his plans for the future.
At the price of great hardships he succeeded in being grad-
uated from his municipal school, where he had the best
marks. Only one week after graduation, he entered a factory as an apprentice laborer, and his family was entirely
dependent upon his meager earnings. "I did not even have
the chance of learning any trade, though I would gladly
have studied to become a skilled worker."

It is not difficult to understand with what hope this father
greeted the birth of his son, and how the boy came to be the
main purpose of his whole life. Even so, the man would

never have spoken of all this, had we not recognized him for what he was and brought him to talk about himself. We also see that his son's refusal to study made this man feel cheated of his last consolation in life; and that he was in no position to recognize his son's incapacity to fulfill his father's ambitions.

This man will have to pay many visits to our child guidance clinic before he accepts the idea that his son is not a continuation of his own being. If we were to stress this obvious point too early in our interviews, he would simply deny it, just as he used to deny it in talking to the schoolteacher, who warned him often enough. Until he has given up his own aim in life, which is so charged with emotion, he cannot bring himself to accept his son as an independent being who must tread his separate path, follow his particular destiny, lead his individual existence.

The first thing in our task is to help the man reach such understanding. This is no mean achievement, and requires much patience and comprehension. In no case are we to rush ahead and attempt to establish a stormy transference during our first interview. On the contrary, things should proceed very slowly. At the beginning, we concentrate entirely on the father, and get him to tell his own story. We show him our complete interest and we accept his interpretations. Even if we differ somewhat in this or that particular, we put it off until later. At this stage we try not to irritate him by contradictions; on the other hand, we must also avoid any attitude which might lead to the formation of a "father-son" or "teacher-student" relationship between us. In fact, we should enable him to retain his full stature and to treat us as an equal; if anything, we would rather have him feel a trifle superior to the social worker. For in that way we provide him with a kind of personal experience which he has always sought, and never found.

As a result, the father is presently coming to visit us quite willingly; he takes obvious pleasure in expressing himself; in short, the transference has taken effect. As soon as we notice this, we alter our behavior; we do not find it so difficult now to convince him that his son is also entitled to an existence which would correspond to his individual needs; and we even bring the father to act accordingly. We achieve the best results by reminding him of his own childhood.

In all cases of this kind we must expect parents to manifest their hatred of the child; indeed, these expressions of hate are sometimes quite extreme. But such reaction is entirely normal, and if it does not arise spontaneously, the counselor should actually provoke it: by this means a real reconciliation between parents and child can take place, and a natural, normal love relationship may begin. We discharge the father and son, and consider their case as finally closed only when the youngster is taken out of school and finds himself a calling to his liking; while his father turns his newly freed libido toward his own field of interests, of course not without guidance from us.

Once alerted to this type of father, we first begin to notice how often we encounter it in our professional work. Of course, we do not always meet this particular situation—to wit, living out some unattainable childhood wishes in the person of his own son, and thus suffering shipwreck—for it is not necessarily one's own child who is the bearer of one's unfulfilled aspirations. In some people, there sometimes persists a tendency to striv efor one's own original goal, be it through some devious bypath.

All of these fathers were undoubtedly gifted children. They were unable to obtain the formal education necessary to reach their imagined aim. Either their own neurotic inhibitions, or the indifference and lack of comprehension of their parents, or sheer economic destitution may have acted as insurmountable obstacles. As things worked out, they were forced to take up some calling not at all to their liking. This naturally made them dissatisfied with their lot and frustrated in their need for social recognition. Necessarily, they must direct their interest toward other fields, which in turn are determined by their own psychic constitution.

Because of their frequency as a type, we shall deal for the moment with only such fathers as are characterized by a special craving for appreciation and who therefore seek out those social circles which may give them "standing" without inquiry into their educational background. One finds such men in every newly arisen movement, working selflessly, diligently, and enthusiastically; they need not be in the first ranks nor in a leading position, but at least someone should notice them and recognize their performances, or else they will run away. When that happens, they are likely to be indignant for a while, but not disillusioned or actually embittered. On the contrary, they start anew, somewhere else, with the same enthusiasm—perhaps only to suffer once more the same fate. Thus they always march onward. They are generally well liked and warmly regarded, for they stand in nobody's way. But sometimes they become unpleasant through their ceaseless high-pressure attitudes and criticism: things are progressing too slowly for them, everyone is working too little, people around them are too selfish. Should there be no "movement" available for a man of this type, then he expends his energies in clubs and fraternities. The aim of whatever society he may have joined is not the decisive element for him. What he is looking for is merely a field of activity wherein he may find, at long last, that recognition of which he dreams. Such people, who always want to achieve something for themselves while working for the community, are found typically in political life.

Estimates of this sort of person are quite contradictory and depend entirely on the standpoint of the observer. Within the family he may seem good for nothing; outside the family he commands high regard. He is always busy, he worries all the time about other people, but these other people are seldom his closest relatives. The center of gravity of his life does not lie within the family, but he does not realize this at all. He is quite convinced that he is a good man who does not consciously and intentionally neglect his folks; he simply has no time left for them. He completely fails to understand that his kin also want him for themselves.

In his own opinion, he is doing everything for them, and they will share in the recognition and honors he will receive. He thrusts upon his wife the burden of managing the family, agrees with everything she does, never contradicts her —but, on the other hand, she may never lay any claim to him. She must arrange everything by herself, gets no support from him, feels neglected; and withal, she cannot defend herself by calling her husband irresponsible, because he is actually doing everything he can. It is all the fault of the circumstances. Thus the situation remains unchanged, the children become wayward, and the family falls to pieces.

With this type of father, the child guidance worker does not find it difficult to induce transference by the usual methods; nor does he need any greater exertions when it comes to severing this relationship. And yet the task which must be accomplished in the meantime, the solution of the critical home situation, will be tedious and disappointing, unless we know how to make the man change his interests. The great difficulty lies in the fact that the father understandingly agrees with everything the counselor says, and even seems ready to do what is requested of him. But since he lacks any affective interest in his child, he can cooperate only in a passive, never in an active way. For instance, if we ask him to give up certain things for the child's sake, he is well able to do so, and he actually tones down his own desires. Nevertheless, he is unable to take upon himself any positive part in the upbringing of his children.

A frequent source of conflict is found in those families where there are growing daughters who in their struggle for independence tend to overstep the narrow limits that have been set for them; when they are thwarted, they become aggressive. In their reports to the clinic, the parents invariably interpret such behavior in one way: the daughters are seeking sexual experience. As a matter of fact, the real motives are so manifold that we are not yet able, on the basis of our child guidance practice, to recognize all the existing character types and to describe them exhaustively.

Indeed, in this variegated mass of cases we find side by side the uninhibited, strongly instinctual girl, with but feeble libidinal attachments to objects within the family, and the distinctly inhibited girl, with powerful intrafamiliar fixations. We discover on the one hand a creature who is psychically intact and has no problems; on the other hand, a person craving for the experiences of life. These cases can be subdivided still further, according to circumstances in the home, which may be peaceful or quarrelsome. Equally characteristic are those girls who intend to go their way with great deliberateness, and those who simply deny their ties to their family, in order "to live their own life."

In order to establish the parents' transference to us, we need not be able at the outset to differentiate these various types of children. This will become an essential requirement later on, in the second phase of our work. But it is certainly important to grasp from the beginning, as rapidly and accurately as possible, what is the parents' reaction to the behavior of the daughters.

Let us consider one example: A mother seeks our help because her fifteen-year-old daughter will not stay at home in the evenings, and often comes back only after the front door has been locked for the night. When reprimanded, the girl becomes insolent and obstinate and provokes such ugly domestic scenes that even the neighbors start complaining.

The mother's intense irritation is clear from her own attitude, from the content of her communication, and from the very manner in which she presents them. She feels that her daughter is ill bred, and she is afraid the girl will inevitably get into trouble. The woman is at a complete loss to know what to do to safeguard the child. It does not occur to her to examine whether the conditions at home, or other causes which do not lie in the child herself, have brought about such shocking behavior. All she wants is that her daughter should be a decent girl, who does not give food for gossip among the neighbors. Nothing else interests this mother.

We quickly recognize that we do not want this woman

merely to act out under our guidance. We prefer to approach her by way of her own critical faculty. We accept her therefore in a position of equality, by recognizing her capacity for independent judgment and by tackling the matter according to her own views. We not only listen to her understandingly and share her attitudes toward her daughter's behavior, but we also grasp her own despairing estimate of the situation. It would be quite wrong to try to establish the facts of the case at the very first meeting. That is unessential at this point; what is important is to help this woman form a transference relationship to us. But this can be achieved only if we do not thwart her emotional outbursts, and agree with her. If we behave in this way, she opens up entirely and we come to learn all we need to know. From a description of her daily life, she moves on to an account of her own childhood, and at this point we may safely anticipate that we shall meet with success by using our usual methods.

Indeed, in the course of several meetings, we came to learn the true circumstances obtaining at home: conflict, nagging, and the absence of love have created an atmosphere which makes it understandable that the growing girl wishes to stay at home as little as possible, and seeks instead the company of friends her own age.

We knew it from the very beginning: this mother would have to be brought to the point of seeing her own home and her family life through her daughter's eyes, before we could expect to make her understand her daughter's needs. To bring her to satisfy the needs of her child, we would have to bring about such a change in the artificially created situation—at exactly the right moment—that we could thereafter appear as this young girl's attorney, defending her rights as he sees fit.

## Engaging the Parents' Conscious Ego

Fundamentally different standpoints must govern our activity when we are dealing with nonneurotic parents. The use of a special technique for the establishment of a strong transference now becomes superfluous, because the mutual relationship follows a normal pattern from the beginning. The creation of an artificial relationship is therefore unnecessary. We are primarily concerned with the conscious ego of the parents, and thus we are satisfied when we arouse in them a feeling of trust sufficiently deep for our purposes. We generally achieve this relationship by natural, unemotional behavior, free from any preconceived tendencies. We are not seeking to bring the client into a state of dependency, nor do we wish to place ourselves in a subservient position. On the contrary, we should both remain independent personalities. Consequently, we listen attentively to the description of the crisis at home, and show our interest in such a manner that the parent cannot fail to sense that he is being understood. On the other hand, we wish the parent to recognize, without undue irritation, that we do not share his views. In the course of a smooth and pleasant conversation —perhaps at times interrupted by emotional outbursts on the part of the parents against the child—we take cognizance of all the relevant facts. Here too, however, we are not satisfied merely with associatively presented material. We demand more than that, whenever we have failed to understand anything quite clearly. In other words, we comport ourselves neither as we would toward parents who must be brought to "act out" according to our own will, nor as with those into whose superego we wish to penetrate intuitively. Instead, we encourage a give-and-take discussion, and conclude the meeting with an exchange of views which is as factual as the rest of the conversation.

The complaints we usually hear about are of the following kind: the child has difficulties in school; he shows poor behavior, which is the result of family circumstances; or we are confronted by disquieting symptoms of various types, which mean that the child's development is really endangered. In most instances, the parents provide us with usable observations, which yield a sufficent number of clues for counseling purposes, once the material has been organized, thought over, and supplemented by means of interviews with the child. Giving advice as to how the parents should act, and how the child should be treated at home, is frequently all we need do in order to complete our task.

The parents' relations with us have remained unstrained, and it is entirely up to us whether we wish to maintain such a relationship beyond the counseling phase. Of course we do not terminate it as long as we entertain any doubts about our guidance. Under such conditions, the parents return gladly to inform us about how well things are going at home or in school; or else they let us know that the expected improvement did not occur. They also bring forth new observational data, and we continue to work together until the hoped-for results have been achieved.

Among the parents just described, there is a small group distinguished by special characteristics. These parents seem rather insecure, somewhat reserved, more or less mistrustful and expectant. Before coming to us, they had been to other child guidance clinics, without achieving results; also, they were influenced by other psychological schools of thought, or warned against the psychoanalytic method; and therefore they are prejudiced.

When dealing with this type of parents, we too must be cool, restrained, and matter of fact—a posture which we relinquish slowly. We gladly place our assistance at their disposal, but avoid everything which might create the impression that we are striving to enlist them in the ranks of our clients. We do not let ourselves be drawn into a discussion of the various psychological opinions: neither in general terms, nor concerning the specific case which has brought them to us. It goes without saying that we refrain from all negative criticism of other psychological views. Nor do we praise our own method, even if we are under provocation to do so; for we know very well that this is exactly what our opponent expects us to do. An assenting remark often eliminates such opposition, particularly when it is dropped unexpectedly. We make statements as to the length of treatment required, or as to its success. We refuse to continue if we come to feel during the first meeting that our relationship with the parents has not developed to the required minimum level.

We are not always given an accurate picture of the family emergency. We know there are parents who make exaggerated statements in their presentation of a case, because of their own neurotic relationship to the child. We also know what our attitude is toward such exaggerations. However, it happens also that facts are sometimes intentionally distorted. We are then dealing with conscious tendencies on the part of the parents, with which we will have to cope first, before we decide whether to handle the case at all, and what methods we will choose from among those already discussed, in order to bring the parents into a transference relationship to us.

The distorted accounts of the factual situation involve conscious exaggerations on the one hand, understatements and evasions on the other hand; essential elements are passed over in silence, or veiled in awkward allusions. When faced with reticence and disguise, the experienced and attentive counselor is hard to mislead. He notices in the behavior and verbal mannerisms of the speaker a desire to minimize things, to skip lightly over the essential facts, and to keep silent altogether on the subject of punishable delinquency, especially where juveniles are involved. It is very difficult for the parents to disguise their intentions so completely, from the beginning to the end of an interview, that they are not provoked by the counselor into betraying themselves, often without realizing it. At such moments, one single blunt statement by the worker is usually enough to clear the atmosphere of all those tensions which the client himself must have found difficult to bear. Really dishonest parents are, after all, a rare exception. Perhaps the only cases of parents who actually seek to mislead us are those who have made their children perform work of an illegal nature, or sent them out to beg. Usually, the behavior described is due simply to mistrust, to shame, or to the fear of bringing harm to the child. What we do in such instances is to remind the parents of the purpose of their visit to the clinic; also, without either antagonizing them or making them more reticent, we draw their attention to the fact that our work can be of service only if we are told everything. We calm them with the remark that we are neither police officers nor deputies of the court, and that our only task is to help them, and help their child. In this way, the feelings of mistrust, shame, and fear are overcome, and we have no further difficulties in tackling the substance of the case.

We would be misled if we mistook an exaggerated description for the actual picture of the critical situation. It becomes most unpleasant for us if we notice, too late, that we have been intentionally misled by parents who wanted to use us for purposes of their own. Since the work done to that point was based on false premises, it is useless. Now we run the risk of becoming ridiculous, of making enemies, and even of harming our clinic as an institution, when we proceed to do what we unfortunately must do: refuse continued collaboration.

We avoid these pitfalls if we listen to the parents' presentation with sharpened attention—so as to let them make ever greater exaggerations, by remaining ourselves passive and expectant throughout. The greater the exaggerations, the more transparent they become.

We do not seek to establish the usual relationship with these parents; nor do we try to make the child comprehensible to them. We know from experience that such an attempt will fail, because the parents will yield to other and stronger interests. We do stress our standpoint as the child's attorney. At that point we do not want to be anything else, and then we leave it up to them to recognize us as a child guidance counselor, or to reject our help altogether.

We deal with cases of parents who are forced by economic necessity to have their children cared for elsewhere, or whose children represent in one way or other an obstacle to their parents. Widowers intending to remarry may find that their intended spouse rejects the children of the first marriage. Divorced parents, or parents engaged in divorce proceedings, may seek to mislead us in the so-called "fight over the children," or rather to make use of us for their own special interests. We must realize that in these struggles, often conducted with the greatest selfishness and brutality, the child's welfare becomes wholly subordinated to the intention of wounding the other party as deeply as possible.

OCCASIONAL PSYCHOANALYTIC ASSISTANCE DURING THE
GUIDANCE PERIOD

In the practice of child guidance, there also arise situations in which it does not suffice that we inject our own personality, as a substitute and an object of transference, into the libidinal structure of a family; or that we cause the parents to act out according to our plans; or that we tackle directly their conscious tendencies. Sometimes it becomes necessary to use means which are truly psychoanalytic, so as to make conscious the parent's conflicts and interpret them correctly. We thus hope to achieve more than with those methods described. Whatever knowledge the counselor needs for such "psychoanalytic child guidance," he learns from the analysis of the neuroses. We mention a few typical histories, in order to give the child guidance worker at least an idea about what cases may fall into this category.

Parental jealousies give us the most trouble in this connection: jealousy of the father, or the mother, focused either upon a social worker who acts as a marriage counselor, or upon the children themselves. It is frequently impossible to decide at first sight whether we are dealing with reactions grounded in natural human behavior, or with the ultimate outcome of paranoid conditions which we cannot hope to master. Despite the risk, we cannot avoid tackling emergencies which might in fact have a paranoid basis.

A few examples follow of the kind we meet most frequently.

In fathers who torment their child with jealousy, this tendency grows markedly stronger if the child is in fact more loved by his mother, or if, because of his innate capacities, he may be expected to achieve more than his father. The most severe conflicts arise between parent and child, and therefore the gravest emotional crises when the mother is not aware of her husband's jealousy, or in cases where she intentionally refuses to concede the father's position of leadership within the family. When this occurs, the father engages in downright persecution of his child.

Mothers who are jealous of their growing daughters, either toward the father, or still more frequently toward the stepfather, cannot reconcile themselves with the loss of their own femininity; they cling abnormally to their husbands; they try exaggeratedly to limit his freedom of action, and often rob him of opportunity to exchange a few loving words with his own child; they observe suspiciously every gesture made by husband and daughter, and then discharge their dissatisfaction upon the daughter alone. Consequently, the girl feels still more drawn toward her father or stepfather. Family life becomes impossible, the more so because the girl is intolerant of her mother and uses every opportunity to withdraw from the domestic environment; a reaction which exposes her to the dangers of waywardness.

Some stepmothers who for conscious reasons have given up the idea of having children of their own, in order to devote themselves entirely to the upbringing of their husband's child by his first wife, but now are motivated by a belated, not always consciously recognized jealousy, so that they actually defend the rights of their own unborn offspring against the pretensions of the "strange" child. The consciously loving behavior of the stepmother may manifest itself in such an overburdening of the child that he feels the unconscious urge to react contrary to every expectation, thus unwittingly provoking still greater manifestations of love. In other words, stepmother and stepchild do not understand each other. As to the father, he stands by helplessly, torn

between the two beloved persons of his own family. Whenever there is conflict at home, he feels so insecure that he
must continually shift his position, backing first the one
party, then the other, then the first one again, with the result that both the wife and his child fail to appreciate his
intentions and eventually reject him. A critical situation
finally arises, and the stepmother interprets it as due entirely
to the child, while the child feels it is the fault of his stepmother.

Other stepmothers are jealous of the deceased wife, because
the first wife seems to be the preferred one, either in fact or
only in the imagination of the stepmother. Trouble often
arises usually because of photographs, or personal belongings
of the deceased. These things which are preserved out of
genuine reverence or out of sheer carelessness will get on
the nerves of the stepmother. She strives at first (either lov-
ingly or energetically) to establish for herself that position
which, in her opinion, belongs to her and not to the dead
wife. This is something she cannot achieve all at once, however, and her attempts are premature: they come at a time
when the husband and children are not yet able, inwardly,
to meet her wishes. Meanwhile, the stepmother reacts with
bitterness. The members of the family do not understand,
they too become angered, and the stepmother's demands are
rejected. This is enough to create a very critical situation,
which from then on deteriorates until those unavoidable conflicts arise which lead to an emergency within the family.

We are confronted with so many forms of the stepmother
problem, that it might be worth while to study this material
from the standpoint of psychoanalysis. For our present purpose it is sufficient to say that a family life proceeds relatively more smoothly, with fewer conflicts, if a man's second
marriage is also blessed with offspring, than if the stepmother brings her own children into her new home, or
renounces having children of her own, or fails to have children, although she wants them. It seems that the relationship
of the spouses requires offspring with the force of an ele-

mental necessity, and that disturbances are bound to arise (which unavoidably involve any stepchildren) if nothing is done to meet this elemental, unconscious need. Experience has shown that even the best intention and conscious efforts can do nothing to counteract these natural trends.

Though much has been said or written about the "evil stepmother," she does not appear more frequently in actual life than the bad mother. But the growth of the evil stepmother concept has been made possible by the manifestation of other unconscious conflicts which have been misinterpreted.

Interpretation is difficult in cases where the mothers live out, in the child himself, their disturbed love relationship to the father, though unconscious of it.

A pregnant girl marries the father of her child only for reasons of practical or moral convenience, despite the fact that she has become indifferent to him, or vice versa. This child is not the hoped-for blessing of a union, nor is he the fulfillment of an unconscious wish fantasy. (Such fantasies do in fact occur, but lead to disturbances of a different kind.) The child now becomes merely a burden, an unpleasant responsibility, a duty which would be irksome if the parents were conscious of their dislike for the child. However, the mechanism of repression leads actually to such love manifestations as must force the child into abnormal channels of development, since the child senses, correctly, that these manifestations are really the outcome of rejection, of an unconscious lack of love.

An unmarried mother is abandoned by the father of her child, marries another man, and brings her own child into her husband's home. No new children result from this marriage. The husband loves his wife, and even his stepchild, quite tenderly; and the wife too is convinced that she cares deeply for her spouse, even though she hardly expects him to fulfill her own deepest longings. She is therefore surprised at the many quarrels which continually arise, involving both husband and child. Although her husband keeps giving in and tries to keep peace, while she herself is careful not to give grounds for displeasure, the clashes grow more frequent and bitter. The child is of paramount importance to her (or so she thinks), yet she often mistreats him. She does not understand her own actions, and this frightens her. She goes on experiencing this ambivalence, centered on the lost object of her former love, and thereby endangers her marriage, destroys the domestic harmony and the child's future as well.

Let us examine two more cases.

The first involves a family where the mother feels she has lost caste. As a young girl, she married beneath her station. After the period of sexual overvaluation had ended, she found herself tied up with a socially incompatible companion. A feeling of discomfort gave way to actual distaste. At present she treats her husband without consideration and is increasingly unhappy because she meets with no understanding of her plight. As to the man, he finds himself in a similar situation. Coming from a different social environment, his outlook on life, his habits, his means of expression, his ways of satisfying his needs, differ radically from those of his wife. The marriage becomes more and more a failure, with all the unavoidably damaging consequences for the youngsters in the family. It is questionable whether any interpretative work can solve the problem in these situations, or whether the emergency is already such that a remedy is possible only with the help of a more radical analysis.

The second case is that of the family with the ambitious mother. A gifted, self-conscious girl marries while still very young; her husband is a capable, but not very active man. In time, she finds that she has failed to reach the position in life of which she had dreamed, and that the fault lies with her husband who is not able to make an adequate career. She now becomes active, meddles in her husband's business, offers suggestions, makes claims, prods him ceaselessly, without noticing that all her activity is only making her husband still more retiring, still more incapable of meeting the everyday requirements of his occupation. She undertakes the education of her children with the same zest, and differs with the father and the child in her estimate of each child's capabilities. Whenever she meets with failure, she blames not only the members of her own family for their incapacity but also, quite frequently, the ill-will and maliciousness of strangers. The perpetual activity and restlessness of this mother inhibit the children's development, incite the husband to resistance, or drive him to resignation. Finally, the youngsters have to be brought to the child guidance clinic, with complaints of neurotic disease and of poor performance in school.

In the cases so far described, with the single exception of the last one, we have shown what kind of guidance should be offered and what treatment applied. As to the last instance, we have nothing to add which a psychoanalytically trained counselor does not already know. From such experience as he has gained in treating neuroses, he well understands how a transference can be achieved, and how it should be dissolved again; how the unconscious material is made conscious, and how these data are to be interpreted. For this reason, we limited ourselves to a presentation of the central family conflict, which to the psychoanalyst is immediately recognizable as an irruption of the repressed.

THERAPEUTIC RESULTS OF QUESTIONING

We have learned from experience that an educational emergency sometimes disappeared after a single visit to the child guidance clinic. No further difficulties were encountered with the children, and the domestic conflict seemed to have been eliminated. Inquiries made after several years tended to substantiate these successes. While we realize full well that a single interview could not have brought about a cure in the psychoanalytic sense, we were often satisfied with such positive results; only a very small proportion of the disturbances brought before us could have been subjected to analytic treatment.

These cases failed to attract our attention for a long time, as we heard of the favorable outcome only at a later date, when we happened to visit the families in question. Until then, we were rather of the opinion that the parents had been dissatisfied for some reason unknown to us, and therefore had not returned a second time to the clinic. It was only later that we tried to find an explanation for such surprisingly lasting results which our relatively short interview seemed to have obtained.

It would be uninteresting to describe one of these interviews in detail; indeed, it would serve no purpose because nothing much occurs in such conversations. The essential elements must be looked for elsewhere. The experienced counselor takes the flow of words spoken by his client as a stream of free associations; meanwhile he thinks of the child with his conflicts, and he sees the behavior of the parents—derived from their own childhood experiences. In assessing the character of the parents, the counselor is interested not so much in the content of infantile conflicts, as he is in the resulting unconscious attitude of these parents toward their own parents, and the manner in which they now externalize this attitude as adults, in their relations with their children. This is because of the compulsion to repeat.

To work in this manner, a counselor needs experience, which enables him to classify individuals—without knowing their particular conflicts—into certain approximate types. If he is able to grasp at once the correct state of affairs, he may then by means of an indirect question block the existing channels which serve as outlets for repressed emotions.

An example will suffice to clarify the procedure. There is a family where life is being increasingly disrupted by the recurrently brutal behavior of the father. His daughter, although strongly attached to him, comes to reject him more and more as she grows up. She controls herself very well, because more than anything else she hates rudeness, in whatever form and from whatever source. She behaves, at first consciously, later on through sheer habit, in a manner exactly opposite to that of her father. But she does not suspect that her "brutal father" is very much alive in her own character, she is ready to spring into action whenever she fails to keep her emotions under intellectual control. When she gets married and becomes a mother, her peculiar psychic make-up acquired in her adolescence turns out to be harmful to her own child. Indeed, her behavior is marked by such contrasts that the child must perforce suffer. Phases of extraordinary gentleness are followed suddenly, whenever she gets angry, by indescribable fits of brutality, which remain quite incomprehensible to the child. The defensive attitudes of the child and the reactions of the mother produce most serious difficulties in the child's rearing.

At the right moment and in a seemingly casual manner, the counselor asks her: "Was your father a very brutal man?" This simple question provokes the desired reaction on the part of the mother—a reaction which is far-reaching in scope; a lasting success is thereby achieved, and the task of the child guidance worker completed.

What happens within the mother's psyche at such a time? Since nothing had heretofore been said of her father, the woman's ego marvels at the omniscience of the counselor, which she now thinks extends to everything pertaining to her personality. The ego is deceived by this illusion; the transference is reinforced, and the counselor becomes a magician, who is not only admired but feared. As the question was asked within the context of her report about the difficulties with her child, her own superego is now warned: "What your ego does is connected with your libidinal relationship to your father—whom you reject, after all." Thus, that channel is blocked which served as an outlet for the repeated explosions of the woman's id.

In the light of our psychoanalytic experience, we may deem it strange indeed that one single question should have such a sustained effect, particularly because common daily practice has shown us how many months of work are usually required to open any new outlets for the id. However, the effect becomes more comprehensible when we consider what would have happened if we had taken pains to interpret to the mother the riddle of her behavior and tried to make her conscious of those connections of which we are aware. Had this been done, the entire critical faculty of the ego would have been awakened and its power of resistance brought into play; and thus a situation of antagonism would have arisen between us and the mother, which would have required several months of tedious work to resolve—provided that the mother would have come back to the clinic.

The entire success seems to consist in the mere fact that we had succeeded in warning the ego. Presumably, we thereby strengthened the ego's defenses against the unconscious, and interrupted the previously available channel of discharge. The mother probably will replace the old symptoms (the outbreaks of brutality) with some other symptomatic manifestations. But this bothers us very little, if at all, for we are primarily interested in eliminating those factors which have become harmful to the child's development.

From this experience we have gained a general principle for the technique of child guidance, a principle valid in certain well-defined situations. Let us enunciate it in the following manner. What we want to know must be asked indirectly, in a way that places the ego of the patient in a state of tension—a state with which the ego is unable to cope, and which it escapes only by avoiding the critical situation altogether, or by acting out in accordance with the counselor's will.

A similar procedure of questioning is to be recommended also in cases where the complaining parent happens to be the cause of the conflict which forms the storm center of his disturbed family life; and where a radical change in his behavior at home would make the domestic conditions more tolerable. But the counselor will try to provoke such change in behavior only if he is convinced that the father possesses those inner capabilities needed for any far-reaching readjustment.

What decisive effects may thus be set in motion can be seen from the following case. A woman comes to the clinic and denounces her husband for having reprehensible relations with his own daughter. But the counselor soon recognizes that this incest committed by the husband is caused solely by his wife's behavior. He therefore refrains from pressing any formal charges against the man. Instead, during one of the interviews with the woman, he brings about such a situation in her psyche that her husband is now enabled to achieve a normal sexual relationship with her, therewith giving up his unnatural liaison with the daughter.

In exceptional cases, a single direct question may suffice to resolve the conflict at hand. We can think of no better illustration than the following.

A society lady, a foreigner, comes to us with the request of helping her daughter, who, in her own words, has fallen ill with severe melancholia. She describes the girl's condition in such terms that one must assume a really grave sickness. As a rule, the child guidance clinic does not handle cases of melancholia; but before advising the mother to go to a psychoanalyst, we prefer to gather some additional information. We therefore invite the daughter to come and see us. She enters the office in complete silence; silently, she sits down in front of the counselor; and several minutes elapse before this silence is broken.

Then the child guidance worker begins to talk:

"It will be no fun if we go on staring at each other without speaking. Though I can well imagine that you don't have much to tell to a complete stranger."

The girl keeps silent and seems utterly unconcerned.

"I want to make you a proposal," says the counselor again. "Try to imagine something, anything at all, which happened some time ago. You needn't even tell me about the particular thing you'll have recollected. This is surely not a dangerous proposal. Do you agree?"

"Yes."

"Can you imagine something?"

"Yes."

"Now please recall to your mind something that happened about two years ago. Can you think of it?"

"Yes."

"Again, you need not tell me about it. But between these two recollections there must exist some relationship. You just could not think of absolutely anything you wanted. Do you find any such relations?"

"None."

"But you should!"

"And I say no."

"I am curious to find out who is right, you or I. Perhaps you would agree to tell me what you had imagined?" (The counselor is merely anxious to prod the girl into talking.)

"All right."

"What are these two recollections of yours?"

"Six weeks ago, my uncle's senior secretary told me that she has a daughter who is sexually frigid. And two years ago, there was a young man who wanted to kiss me, but I didn't let him."

"So you see, there is a connection between the two things which you had in mind!"

"What connection?"

"The sexually frigid daughter of your uncle's secretary, and you yourself, the girl who does not let herself be kissed."

"Oh, but I did not remember the secretary because of her daughter, but because I have some money accounts to settle with her."

"Are you employed by your uncle?"

"No. I only carry his money orders to the post office and then I settle the accounts with his senior secretary."

"Are you paid for this service?"

"No."

"Does your uncle give you pocket money?"

"No."

"Do you receive your pocket money from your mother?"

"No, I have no money at all. In fact, I have only debts."

"To whom do you owe money?"

"To a girl, a friend of mine."

"What is the amount of your debt?"

"Three hundred shillings."

"For what purpose did you borrow it?"

"To pay a physician's fee."

"But why didn't you ask the father of your unborn child to pay for this operation?"

The girl is quite horrified by this question, and asks in utter amazement:

"How did you know?"

"You have just told me as much."

"But I did not say a single word about the entire business!"

"Yes, you did. A girl of your social class who borrows three hundred shillings from a friend for medical purposes does so only when she is in no position to reveal to her own family the reason of her visits to the doctor. Obviously, you were forced to consult a gynecologist."

The girl, who is sobbing bitterly, now makes a full confession. It appears from her own story that both the pregnancy and the abortion were lived down quietly, without excitement. But at present, that is several months afterwards, the friend from whom the girl had borrowed money is pressing for a prompt repayment of the debt. The girl finds herself at a loss as to how to procure this amount, and actually contemplates taking the three hundred shillings from the sums which she is supposed to pay in at the post office; she would then pretend to have lost the corresponding sum. However, there is a hitch: while she could get away with it as far as her uncle is concerned, the lie would be easily detected by his senior secretary.

The necessity of repaying the debt, the impossibility of getting money by honest means, the dreadful alternative of either embezzling the funds or failing to repay anything, the inner debate, with its seesaw of pros and cons, put the unfortunate girl into a mood which her mother interpreted wrongly as melancholia, because she did not know the facts of the case.

Our question, "But why didn't you ask the father of your unborn child to pay for this operation?" acquired such a decisive significance not only because it showed the girl clearly that we understood the true state of affairs, but also because this sudden remark, sprung at her as a complete surprise, brought her a sense of relief in the very midst of her shock and fear. Indeed, the girl had no longer any confession to make; she was merely asked to confirm a fact which had already been implicitly admitted.

Not every situation where circumstances are falsely represented lends itself to this type of procedure. We become aware of the possibilities inherent in this method only in such instances where we definitely perceive the existence of conscious feelings of guilt, or the symptoms of depressive behavior. At first we are not yet sure whether the truth is really being withheld from us; perhaps we cannot even assume that there is sufficient cause for telling lies to the counselor. And therefore we cautiously attempt to provoke an extremely detailed and all-embracing statement concerning this acute conflict. With a little shrewdness and talent, any experienced worker will soon be able to arrive at some definite conclusions as to the crux of the matter. He will then discover the real misdeed, or at least that action which the subject's own superego considers as punishable.

But a child guidance worker who happens not to possess the somewhat special gifts required on such occasions would do well if he renounced altogether any attempt at solving problems by this method. For indeed, a "near miss" would not yield any positive result, and might even cause considerable damage.

## The Child Guidance Worker and the Children

### ESTABLISHING A POSITIVE TRANSFERENCE:
### GENERAL CONSIDERATIONS

In the preparatory phase of treatment, the positive transference of the parents is more important than that of the child. However, inasmuch as the difficulty is determined by the condition of the child himself, one cannot start solving this educational crisis unless and until there have arisen some fairly strong emotional ties between the counselor and the child. This statement is also valid in other forms of pedagogic work.

From a certain point on, therefore, we devote ourselves to the child much more so than we have done previously; we try to attract his attention increasingly to ourselves, and we strive to develop whatever friendly relationship already exists, until it reaches the desired strength. This would not be difficult if the children brought to us were coming from families with an undisturbed structure, and had suffered only minor disturbances in the development of their own libido organization. It would then be quite enough to treat the child kindly, according to his instinctual demands, without unduly stressing a benign attitude. Indeed, the child would already be familiar with it, and would react favorably, because of his previous experience with his parents.

But there hardly exists a single wayward child who comes from a well-ordered family background, even though it may appear normal from the outside.

Our previous examples may already have shown how harmful the family can become, either through an excessive concern for the child or, on the contrary, by too frequent frustration.

Yet there are family circumstances, similar to those described, or even much more harmful, wherein the child succeeds in resolving acute conflicts—and resolves them in an ego-syntonic and reality-adapted way. He develops normally and does not become delinquent. An abnormal development occurs only when there is a second factor that influences unfavorably the growth of the child; to wit, when as a result of his own inner disturbances the child can no longer find any satisfactory way to reconcile the requirements of external reality with the demands of his own ego, and when these two pressures have become mutually incompatible.

The study of delinquency has made us aware of the fact that in every case of waywardness the child's erotic life has been disturbed at an early infantile stage: the relationship to the parents has somehow become abnormal, and the original relations of the children to one another, strained as they are by competition, have not developed into a normal brotherly bond, as they should have if they had been submitted to the influence of an equally divided affection toward the parents. Moreover, such a child has experienced repeated disappointments, because his need for love has never been satisfied, and rejection has become more and more unbearable.

After long experience with juvenile delinquents, we deem it important to set apart one particular type within the general category of wayward children whose delinquency is due to too little pressure from the parents.

There is an unavoidable minimum of frustration in the rearing of any child; but there are a few children who react to this minimum in a manner so excessive, that it would seem to be maximum. This extraordinary reaction is probably due to the excessive and early fixation of a component instinct in the child.

If the person who bring up such a child happens to be of a similar type, he will intuitively grasp the child's psychic situation correctly and try to meet it by diminishing the outside pressure; whereupon, contrary to expectation, the child becomes wayward.

As seen by observers in the environment of the child, it would appear that this faulty development is due to insufficient restriction of the instinctual life, and to excessive fulfillment of instinctual desires. This uninhibited gratification of the instincts, which come into perpetual conflict with reality, has caused the inner conflicts which bring the child into aberrant paths.

From the subjective viewpoint of this type of child, whatever license is granted him still seems too little, so that these children, like others, suffer from an excess of frustration.

The continuing disappointments and the complete inability to master the resulting inner conflicts lead to repeated failures in the regulation of libidinal trends, and thus an important part of the preparation for later life has miscarried. The child never arrives at those object-libidinal cathexes which, through their later continuous repetition, would have led to normal relationships. Furthermore, the child's own libidinal anticipatory ideas depart from normalcy to such an extent that there is a great uncertainty in his relations to persons in his environment. Also, in certain cases, there are additional disturbances—due to a return of the child's libido to his own ego.

All children of this particular type come to the clinic with their total personalities injured, both by internal and external factors.

The psychoanalytically trained child guidance worker discovers without difficulty whether a crisis in the child's development is caused by a childhood neurosis or psychosis; and he knows how to act and what to prescribe. On the other hand, he is aware that there is no comprehensive description of well-defined clinical pictures from the immensely variegated forms of delinquency. We admit that we understand the causes of delinquency only in general terms; we have scarcely reached the point where we can establish the details of individual causal connections; and we are still further from a systematic comprehension of etiological factors.

We are perhaps able to draw certain general conclusions from the type of manifestations in which delinquency expresses itself. But we are in no position to state, with any degree of precision, what are the particular disturbances in the child's erotic life, and what are the specific reactive formations in response to frustrations, which must underly latent states of delinquency which precede each case of manifest waywardness. Nor can we say what precipitating cause brought about the actual manifestation of delinquency.

Even if these problems were solved, this would still not be

enough to provide us with valid rules for the establishment
of a transference in each individual case. It would enable us,
however, to start researches which would make it ultimately
possible for the child guidance worker to conduct himself
correctly, according to plan, at each particular phase of the
child's development. Beyond this, the counselor must still
take into consideration the special position of the child at
the clinic: children do not come of their own free will; they
are compelled by their parents. Often, they have intimidated
the children before bringing them to us. We turn our initial
attention to the parents, rather than to the children, for
reasons we have explained.

It is therefore easy to understand that instructions about
the technique of establishing transference can only be of a
general nature.

The task of creating a positive emotional relationship to
ourselves is definitely more difficult with children or youngsters than with parents.

The parents come with the conviction that they have
always wanted and done only what was best for their children. They often feel that they have sacrificed themselves for
the little ones; but that now, instead of being rewarded by
well-behaved, obedient, thankful boys and girls, they get
nothing but worry, toil, and vexation. They consider themselves misunderstood, offended, wronged, badly treated, and
injured by their own children.

These parents have become powerless and they need our
help. Their conscious attitude toward us is therefore never
rejection; they are in a psychic state appropriate for achieving a positive transference.

The initial situation of the parents differs substantially
from that of the children. If the wayward youngsters have
been intimidated and are now overcome by anxiety, they see
in us only a tool of their parents and will have nothing
to do with us. They are disagreeable, either in a subtle or in
a quite outspoken manner; they may be stubborn, tearful,
or incipiently aggressive, depending upon their level of de-

velopment, the psychic condition in which they happen to be, and the milieu to which they belong. Sometimes we do not interest them in the least; they are bored, it is hard to get them to talk, and they clearly let us understand that they prefer to get away as soon as possible. In other instances, they behave like "wise guys," always trying to act smartly and to impress us accordingly. The whole spectrum of possible attitudes, either childish or spuriously adult, spreads itself before our eyes. As a rule, however, these youngsters try to conceal what they are really like; they misrepresent themselves and they tell lies, in a clever or clumsy manner; often their silly tricks are at once recognizable, but not infrequently they act with such refined cunning that we are not able to penetrate their disguise.

Yet this behavior is understandable. To these children we appear as representatives of society at large, and as such we seem to be their opponents; they hardly expect any help from us. It is only much later that they recognize their error. In the meantime, they must avoid showing us any weak spots, and they conduct themselves with the greatest caution. The strength of the delinquent lies precisely in his capacity for deceiving the adversary. For that reason, in severe cases of waywardness, the youngster shows himself modest and submissive, deceitfully friendly, and overflowing with pretended righteousness.

It is crucially important to form immediately a correct estimate of the attitude taken by the child. It is essential that the transference be established quickly, if possible during the very first interview. We are often called upon to take certain steps after the first meeting, or after the first few meetings, and our position is therefore one of emergency. We must work fast. We need that sort of experience which enables us to evaluate correctly the character of the child, even when he is trying to deceive us by insincere and artificial behavior. For it is only after we have perceived his true nature that we can start to make him emotionally dependent upon us.

This form of child guidance should be undertaken only by people who have gained sufficient prior experience in the handling of delinquents. For it is only after we have perceived the delinquent's true nature that we can start to make him emotionally dependent upon us. This form of child guidance requires sufficient prior experience, for it is through actual field work with wayward children, and not in the guidance clinic, that one learns something about their psychic structure and their needs.

In the first part of this paper the importance of an immediate transference relationship with the parents was emphasized. In working with juveniles (children, and even more so, adolescents), this short moment of first contact seems to us even more essentially significant. Most juvenile delinquents meet us at first with utter distrust, and their suspicions must be swiftly overcome before we can win them over. Such suspiciousness is not in any way pathological; the child guidance clinic appears as something dangerous to him; we are strangers, and he is convinced that we will harm him. In keeping with the unpleasant experiences he has had so far with adults, he is entitled to expect something distasteful. Yet he is used to finding himself in dangerous situations, and he can render them harmless if only he sizes them up quickly and correctly. The faster he orients himself, the faster he masters the situation, and the less trouble befalls him. He therefore feels immediately compelled to consider the personality of the counselor carefully, right from the moment he enters the office at the clinic.

We too try to discern as quickly as possible who it is we are dealing with, and both of us strive for ascendancy. There ensues a contest. We try to win mastery over the wayward child, while he puts up a resistance, without actually clashing with us. Many conscious and unconscious mechanisms are involved in the process of the struggle. One senses what is going on, without really knowing much about it.

The juvenile delinquents do not always approach us in this mood of aggressiveness. If the wayward youngster behaves differently, then we accommodate ourselves and observe any further changes in the child's conduct. As a rule, we greet him without saying a word, and with only a glance and a handshake which show him clearly, or at least allow him to sense, our own friendly intentions. The enquiring glance is sometimes followed immediately by a helpful remark; or often by a question, asking him whether he knows who we are. We at once banish his doubts and make him aware that he has nothing to fear from us. Meanwhile an affectionate remark will have started us off on our acquaintance. When we deal with the "wise guy" type, we allow ourselves to be duly impressed, if we think that this might facilitate our relationship; or, on the contrary, we demonstrate our superiority at once, if we want to irritate him intentionally. As to the stubborn child, or the child who is frightened and intimidated, we meet him with patience and friendliness, and refrain from any display of energy; for we do not want him to start crying, or to become even more obstinate and defiant. With the child given to fantasy, who exaggerates for unconscious reasons or tells lies because of his neurotic condition, we follow him into his imaginary world and do not try to point out the contradictions we discover in his statements. Then there are children who are cautiously crafty, or who act as they do for quite intentional purposes: they misrepresent or distort the facts, so as to lead us astray. With these, if we want to make them feel safe, we behave in such a way as to let them believe, at first, that they have fooled us; conversely, if we want them to become anxious, we simply allow them to understand that we have seen through their schemes. Some children have a sense of safety ("Nothing can happen to me") from their nursery days, because if one of the parents happens to forbid something, the child evades the prohibition merely by running to the other. Some children can escape the demands of reality because they are supposedly in a "nervous" condition. In dealing with all these latter cases, we do not, at the outset, put up any resistance against the child. We shall have occasion to speak of this matter later on.

In whatever way our interview may develop, we never

allow the children to stand in our presence; we insist rather that they be seated. We always address the younger children immediately in the direct second person [German *Du,* corresponding to old English *thou*]; with adolescents we postpone this more familiar form of address until the transference is well established.

We always allow the conversation to flow naturally. We try to avoid the attitudes, questions, and answers that smack of formal school discipline. Nor do we let the patient assume the part of a defendant in court. Should it prove difficult for the child to converse in cultured High German, or if his way of talking becomes stilted and affected, we go over to the Viennese dialect. We do not object to any emotional expressions which the child might use in speaking of persons of his own age, or even of parents and teachers; but we refrain from making any comments. As to the general course of the conversation, we behave in the same way as with the parents. We do not try to steer the talk, but let the children speak in whatever manner, and on whatever topic they wish.

Naturally, the concrete content of our questions and remarks is always in line with the peculiarities of the emergency at hand, as well as with the individuality of the child, and his psychic situation at each particular moment. We try to move exclusively within his own circle of interests, and it is only in quite exceptional cases that we start speaking at once about the "offence" which caused him to be brought to the clinic. Usually we deem it preferable that some time should elapse before the child becomes aware of our knowledge of his position.

It is not always easy to get little children to speak, and to win them over. In this respect women counselors are often more clever than their male colleagues. We try to find an opening in childish play, in fairy tales, and in nursery lore. We show our delight in any trinket the child may wear, in a necklace, earring or hairpin, or in a pretty jacket or colorful apron. We may stage an imaginary puppet play with allotted roles, and thus gain some insight into the good or bad relationships of the child to persons in his environment.

During our first contact with schoolchildren, the school itself should usually remain a forbidden topic of conversation. Of course, there are exceptions to this rule: it sometimes happens that a child's life at home is felt as something very distasteful, whereas his school life is pleasant. There are many other areas in which we can willingly follow the child. We thus have sufficient themes to feed our conversation, if we manage it skillfully. However it may be, we treat all of them as adults; we discuss their acquaintances, their boy and girl companions, starting from the general and working our way to particulars: the good friend, as well as the obnoxious girl who likes only gossip and scandal. We also talk about pleasant and unpleasant neighbors, and even touch upon the current fashions in clothing: we allow ourselves to be informed about prices and bargains, about fancy dresses, nice hats, stockings, and the like—always remembering to be duly shocked by their expensiveness, or pleased at their cheapness. Nor do we forget to inquire about a girl's favorite movie star. And if there be other spheres of interest, we readily enter them, to debate for instance about a theatrical play, or any other topic that seems meaningful in the girl's life.

With male adolescents, it is the various sports which usually provide an inexhaustible theme for conversation, with football easily the most popular subject. Skiing finds fewer adepts among juvenile delinquents, because it is too expensive. They like to go bathing and swimming, but are far less commonly ice skaters. Boxing has a great many fans, who display the wildest interest in this sport; whereas the physically weaker youths are fond of jujitsu, because they can imagine themselves in the parts of a gentleman robber or a master detective. We have full-scale debates about the merits of various prominent football players, about current athletic events, and about the fairness or unfairness of the decisions reached by the umpires. We listen to the most emotional descriptions of battles in the ring, and we share the boy's indignation at every improper move made by one of the contestants. We listen with good grace to a youngster's condensed renderings of detective films and crime stories, and we come to know something of his own character in the "heroes" with whom he identifies himself. Moreover, we discuss at great length those plans which the young man has made for his future, and which are, alas, quite impracticable for the most part; we examine painstakingly the prospects of becoming a professional football player, or perhaps a movie actor. More recently, many youngsters introduce the career of pilot into their catalogue of worth-while callings.

Among high school pupils of the upper grades, although they will express themselves with more refinement and restraint, a similar trend can be observed in many cases. One must except, however, those young people who do poorly at school because of neurotic disorders. Their interests are more closely bound with the school, and their expressed desires as to their future professions remain in most cases within the limits of practicability.

### THE CHILD'S CONSCIOUS NEED FOR SUPPORT AND TENDERNESS

In an earlier work (1925), we have sought to establish a frame of reference which would enable us to determine the proper means necessary for the retraining of juvenile delinquents, and would help us find the starting points for curing delinquency more generally. This search has led us to divide delinquents in two categories, according to the results of their upbringing: those who had received too much rearing, and those who had received too little.

For the purposes of our present exposition, however, such classification would be quite unproductive. What we need now is to group the wayward children according to their conscious and unconscious relations with adults, and according to their reaction to unsatisfied needs. We must first determine how we shall proceed in each case at the clinic, according to plan and yet in harmony with the given individuality of the child, so as to awaken in him a feeling of affection toward us, which would lead to a conscious, strongly positive attachment.

When we look at wayward children from this viewpoint, we cannot fail to notice first those whose conscious need for support and tenderness is not satisfied, and for whom therefore the child guidance worker must come to play the part of a substitute parent.

These cases occur frequently in families who live in the worst economic circumstances. The fulfillment of the daily demands of making a living requires so much time and brings such overpowering worries, that the parents cannot devote themselves to their children, even if they wanted to do so. True, the children are not regarded as a burden, and everything required for their basic needs is provided, although at the price of the greatest exertion. But nothing is left over for any other requirements, over and above the barest necessities. If such children are able to understand this situation and if they come to terms with it, then their development may preceed normally even in these unfortunate circumstances. Many a child, however, will take it for granted that parents must strive for the bodily welfare of their offspring; and such a child will demand something more, which is not forthcoming. A crisis may then arise out of these unsatisfied demands. But we cannot hold the parents responsible for it, or condemn them on this score. Indeed, we must blame the unfortunate circumstances: they are such as to subdue even the natural parental love.

In other cases, in which we must likewise take upon ourselves the role of a substitute parent, the economic factors are no longer dominant, or they may even be entirely absent from the problem of upbringing. There are families where the father and mother have each their own field of interests; or if they do have some common interests, these lie entirely outside the family circle. There is, for instance, the father who devotes himself to his club or association, or even more exclusively to politics; or the mother who is more interested in seeing her neighbors, or playing bridge, than in taking care of her children. As to parents who have indeed some pursuit in common, they too may act quite harmfully for their child. Here is one extreme example. A woman brought her three children to the clinic because they could no longer be "controlled" at home. The actual circumstances were the following: her husband, an unemployed mechanic, wanted to get a high school diploma; his wife, who admired him and approved his idea, exerted herself to the utmost in order to provide him with the peace and quiet necessary for his studies—but all this at the expense of the children.

In other families, the relations between husband and wife have cooled off to the point where they have nothing more to share and often nothing even to say to each other. Discussion starts only when the child's behavior becomes strikingly unsatisfactory. Neither the father nor the mother wishes to recognize that the cause of such bad behavior is the loveless atmosphere which prevails in the home.

Often the estrangement goes much further. The parents no longer live side by side, but are pitted one against the other. The child then witnesses at first hand the ugliest kind of daily quarrels, and he cannot take the side of either his father or his mother. At first he does not know what to do, but soon enough he flees the parental home and takes refuge in the street, where he becomes a delinquent.

All these children have one characteristic in common, which sets them definitely apart from those who go astray because their parents are overly concerned with them. Children of the type with which we are now dealing tend to become wayward because no one happens to be sufficiently interested in them.

There is scarcely a single kind of delinquency which might not arise on such a basis. In so far as our work with the child is concerned, the task of establishing a transference and of resolving the problem is relatively easy in these cases. Indeed, it requires no particular technique to effect a transference.

The concrete manifestations of waywardness in these cases are similar to what we observe in other types of delinquency, but they are of a more innocuous character, because the libidinal disturbances have not had so deep an effect.

The difficulties in relieving the disturbance are not so much connected with the child himself; they depend to a greater extent upon his environment. But it is often difficult to introduce any change in this environment. The influence exerted by the counselor on the child alone may prove insufficient to resolve the disturbing situation, and the counselor will have to prescribe the removal of the child from the family. A child guidance worker will recognize soon enough whether this step is necessary, and whether he is able to bring about the resettlement of the child in another home. In fact, the worker's attitude toward the child will depend on this consideration. If he succeeds in having the child placed elsewhere, he will not allow the child's transference to develop beyond a certain point—thus avoiding any additional difficulties connected with the youngster's placement in a new environment. The counselor will proceed with particular caution if he foresees that this change of circumstances will also bring to a stop his own guidance activity. The degree of transference must depend solely on the length of time which the worker expects to devote to the child.

Among the cases to be included in this category, we find most often such children who make themselves unpleasantly conspicuous both in school and at home by not learning their lessons at all, or by preparing them superficially, or by failing to adjust themselves to their classmates, or by playing truant from school altogether. They show little interest and participation in their home life and they meet its daily requirement with passive indifference. Whatever they must do, under pressure from the adults, they do it with obvious unwillingness.

If these children seem to lack zest, it is because there is no one around them for whose sake they might try to cope adequately with the demands of reality; for whose sake they would overcome their own boredom, accomplish their duties, renounce certain pleasurable experiences, and accept a dose of unpleasure.

Usually, we can tell from the behavior of the parents at the child guidance clinic, from their statements about their child, and from their description of everyday events at home whether we have to deal with a case of the type described above. The situation should become entirely clear after a few questions concerning relations between members of the family.

As we have said, we need no particularly developed technique to bring these children into a positive emotional relationship to us, and thus make them dependent upon us. In fact, when the counselor understands the normal need for tenderness in these children, and when he responds accordingly, his main task of guidance is actually accomplished.

At the clinic, we welcome those children in a free and natural way, we behave toward them in the most friendly and kindly manner. We listen sympathetically to their accounts about whatever bothers them, and show that we are duly concerned about the burdens imposed on them at home and in school.

I have described elsewhere (1925) how we enter more closely into the child's concerns, and finally win him over, with the result that he starts to behave properly both at home and in school, and to carry out all his obligations gladly and willingly.

We often achieve spectacular results in a very short time, which indeed is not surprising and should not be credited to anybody as a personal achievement. For, in the final analysis, the child's improved behavior is merely a natural response to such experiences as he would have within any normal, orderly family life.

THE UNCONSCIOUS NEED FOR A PATERNAL AUTHORITY AND FOR AN OBJECT OF IDENTIFICATION.

The situation shapes up in an entirely different manner, and offers much greater difficulties, when we deal with youngsters who live in a state of continuous overt conflict with their environment, because of some unconscious need. In this category belong many diverse forms of aggressive behavior on the part of juveniles of puberty and prepuberty age.

We know this behavior to be nothing more than a rebellion against the father, a rebellion carried on with insufficient means. The youngster comes from one of those families, described earlier, wherein the growing child knows his father in a very unpleasant way, as a brutal weakling; but this distasteful experience overwhelms him only at a certain stage in his development. In a previous phase, the child had identified himself with his father, even with his brutal aspect; later on the father would be consciously rejected. Yet the youngster has always lacked a really masculine object of identification. In view of the familial configuration, we might have expected that the youth would display an overly passive, helpless attitude. Though in fact this type of behavior does occur, it develops only in the presence of still other factors which have a decisively negative influence upon the child's maturation. The frequently encountered "brutal" adolescent experiences the phase of development in which he is brought to our clinic as one of invariably strong emotion, and this fact reveals, at least in part, the source of his aggressive conduct: he has lost intellectual control over his own emotions, and thus the identification with the "brutal" father dominates his behavior.

This psychic structure we can recognize clearly enough from what the parents tell us, prior to our first contact with the youngster, and we prepare ourselves to act accordingly. Yet this structure does not always imply that the youth will behave aggressively when he comes to the clinic. He may take up a quite decent attitude upon entering our office, though he is only waiting for an occasion to show his brutality. There is a readiness to shift toward us that conscious hatred which he feels for his father; and consequently, there always exists an extreme danger of his forming a negative transference to us.

We cannot know in advance the frame of mind in which our juvenile patient will visit our clinic. Therefore, we act in such a way that he simply cannot attack us. Although our entire behavior forces him to acknowledge our superiority, and although he now expects the attack to come from us, this attack does not come. Our words sound much friendlier than anything he had anticipated while on his way to the clinic. On the other hand, we do not show ourselves too engaging, too friendly, too gracious, for he would grow distrustful, or he would regard us as the weaker party, and immediately try to behave brutally. But the attitude which we have chosen throws him off balance, makes him uncertain as to our real intentions. He does not know that by the form and content of our behavior we are intentionally countering the two opposite tendencies at work in him. We leave him in this uncertainty for some time; we achieve this also by means of a casual way of conversing about topics unrelated to the conflict which has brought him to the clinic, topics that interest him only superficially. Later on, at the point where we want to win him over, we agree with whatever he says, we share his views, and finally we appear to be his ally against other people. However, all this is conveyed by our general behavior rather than by any explicit words. We do not borrow the tone of a friend of his own age, nor do we act as if we ourselves were an adult delinquent, nor do we make him feel in any way that we are trying to incite him against his father. In fact, we behave in a manner similar to that we shall describe later on, in detail, when we discuss the treatment of a youthful impostor.

How little the "cowardly father" is repressed in the personality of juvenile delinquents of this type we happened to learn at the clinic, after the memorable events of February, 1934,[1] from youngsters who belonged to a Social-Democratic milieu. These patients were brought to us because of their abnormal aggressiveness toward their own fathers. In one

---

[1] *Editor's Note:* The abortive uprising of the Social-Democratic workers in Vienna against the conservative government of Chancellor Dollfuss.

case, a boy had been so stirred up by his passion that he dared criticize his father openly, and to blame him in the most energetic terms.

One variety of juveniles in this group are not easy to recognize; they carry on the same fight against the father, with the same inadequate means, yet their struggle takes a different form. They are not openly aggressive and brutal; their conduct is more cautious, more insidious and malicious; they are vindictive and cowardly, and they attack in a devious manner, and then only when they feel that they are not endangering themselves. They live out in imagination some portion of their hatred toward the father. The personality structure of these youngsters comes fairly close to that of the neurotic delinquent—which is not characteristic of the type of wayward children described above. This last-described form of delinquency originates essentially in an identification with a father of similar character structure.

To achieve a successful transference with patients of this type is even more difficult than with the others, and requires an even faster orientation at the first meeting. The need of recognizing accurately the psychic situation places a still heavier burden upon the practical experience of the counselor; for it is all too easy to confuse this type of delinquent with others. It is absolutely necessary to grasp in detail the particular defects of such patients, and this means that the counselor must grasp their personality precisely and objectively: not an easy task, because these young people may impress the observer in a quite unpleasant way, and therefore vitiate his judgment. It takes longer to establish any transference relationship with these youngsters, and it is difficult to develop.

However, there are other cases where the unconscious need to identify with a person remains very much alive. In many families, the parents do not agree among themselves on the means of rearing which should be used, whether it should be reward or punishment. The children will always regard the advocate of punishment as the stronger person, and the other as the one who gives in, and therefore usually the weaker. While the parents are not able to hide their differences from him, the child notices very soon that he can gain certain advantages in playing the two adults against each other. In their mutual strife, the parents may forget all about the concrete reason for the struggle. But a child who has learned how to make use of such a situation must necessarily suffer heavy damage in his faculty of adaptation to reality. It is in such circumstances that there develops the type of child whom we have characterized by the phrase: "Nothing can happen to me."

From these familial conditions yet another disadvantage results, wherever the mother happens to be the stronger parent. The weak father then remains quite unsuitable as an object of identification for the boy.

The need of an identification object coincides in many ways with the need for a substitute superego. The father is not only a weakling constantly defeated by the mother; he shows also his dependence upon her every time he has to make up his own mind about anything. He is likewise entirely helpless with his children, and sends them to their mother with any affairs or questions they may bring to him. In fact, he seems happiest when no decisions are required from him. On the other hand, he does not behave with his children as one of their own age group, who should be loved, or at least accepted, as a playmate. If he did, there would appear disturbances of quite another kind.

How can a transference be established in such cases as these? We do not wish to enter into such particulars which must result from the personality of the counselor himself. But this much can be said: the child should experience within the shortest possible time that the personality which now impinges on his life is absolutely competent to make decisions, is self-assured, and proceeds toward the goal with a firm will.

There are also cases of delinquency where the superego of the child lacks certain vital features.

In many families, the parents themselves show defects in

their own superego. The partly antisocial thinking and acting
which result from these defects has an unwholesome influence on the social development of children brought up in
such homes. Through the process of identification with
their parents, the children are bound to acquire a superego
which often differs very sharply from the social ideal. Those
children are psychically healthy. Their delinquency falls
in a social and not in a psychological category. The most
extreme case is that of the child who is reared in a family of
criminals.

The formation of the superego necessarily requires the
cathexis of certain objects, leading to identifications. Considering these requirements, we can understand why it happens that even psychically healthy and normal persons often
fail to develop a well-balanced superego structure. Indeed, a
weak or a defective superego may result in such cases where
the child has not been allowed sufficient time to go through
these psychic processes in a normal way. Normal development is a function of time. Experience has taught us that
those children who were compelled by the circumstances of
their earliest childhood to shift frequently from one foster
home to another could not avoid a faulty development. Consequently, their critical faculty is not sufficient for proper
adjustment to the social order.

In those cases, the task of the child guidance worker does
not consist in guiding the child's further development by
means of a transference to himself. Rather it is his duty to
provide these children, as soon as possible, with a suitable
family environment in some appropriate foster home, in
order to give them a chance to make up what they have
missed. During the time he works with these children, the
counselor must keep the transference down to the barest
minimum required for his work.

TRANSFERENCE IN CASES OF NEUROTIC DELINQUENCY

The forms of neurotic delinquency are so manifold, and
their determining causes so little studied, that any attempt
at curing delinquents according to a methodical plan is still

something extraordinarily difficult. In the clinical pictures of these phenomena of delinquency, neurotic symptoms may manifest themselves to a widely varying extent. Should they be commingled in approximately equal proportions with symptoms of delinquency proper, then our diagnosis will really depend upon our own standpoint—the standpoint from which we consider the wayward child. One and the same individual may then appear as a neurotic delinquent or as a delinquent neurotic. The manner of treating all such cases will differ as much from the technique of psychoanalysis as from the methods of pure pedagogy.

When the neurotic symptoms are strikingly apparent, then our procedures will have to approximate those used in child analysis; whereas if the expressions of waywardness pure and simple are definitely predominant, we shall meet them by using the technique of delinquency analysis.

In each case, the child guidance worker must first of all establish to his own satisfaction the predominant causal basis of the disorder: whether it be neurosis or delinquency. The choice between the two alternatives decisively influences the counselor's attitude in regard to the requirements of transference.

Whenever the wayward patient seems neurotic to a high degree, the child guidance worker proceeds with great caution and slowness in gaining the affection of the child; he remains reserved, not to say passive. But even in those cases where he may foresee in advance the necessity of a delinquency analysis, the counselor would do well in keeping the transference at a minimum; otherwise, the future treatment might be prejudiced by the child's strong attachment to the counselor.

The child guidance worker may increase the intensity of the transference only in such cases where the expressions of waywardness remain fairly mild, and where he is therefore able to treat them within the framework of pure child guidance.

As a rule, children who are neurotically delinquent show

symptoms of the following kind: poor progress at school, difficulties in adjusting to life with classmates; overindulgence in daydreams; thefts of a rather harmless nature; the tendency of withdrawing from reality and from the company of people; neurotic reactions after transgressing the prohibition against masturbating.

When such children are brought to our clinic, their first reception should be markedly warm and friendly. But our further attitude must perforce remain passive as long as we do not know whether we will undertake the treatment of the child. In fact, we behave very much like normal, reasonable parents, when they listen to the wishes and take account of the needs of their children, without as yet committing themselves. It is only later, when the child has been accepted as our patient, that we modify our conduct in accordance with the new situation; though even now we remain watchful, taking notice in due time of a child's tendency to include our person in the sphere of libidinal objects within his family. We must thwart this tendency, though we might otherwise expect success because of the well-known compulsion to repeat. We also mark a child's masochistic or sadistic need, whenever his unconscious guilty feeling drives him to confess or to crave punishment. We meet all such inclinations halfway, without giving complete satisfaction to anything. We succeed in doing so by choosing a particular way of talking to the child, both as to content and form, as well as by an appropriate general behavior, which has been already indicated above.

Our concrete procedure with children showing certain typical forms of neurotic delinquency I have discussed elsewhere (1925).

How to keep such cases under observation? It often happens that we are unable to determine with sufficient clarity, in the first interview, the real causes of the family crisis; we then prescribe a period of observation. If the observer sits down with the child and engages him in lengthy, repeated conversations, in order to gain more insight into the problem which still baffles us, he would actually run the risk of making any later psychoanalytic treatment considerably more difficult, if such treatment were to prove necessary at a further stage. Indeed, the observer does not cause any unconscious material to become conscious; his task is not to work like a psychoanalyst. Yet the child, who cannot be expected to make any distinction between observation and analytic treatment, will eventually find himself in a state of mind with which the psychoanalyst may not be able to cope. We should therefore arrange that the observation be done in a way to avoid these unpleasant consequences and still obtain the desired information. What we need to know first and most of all is how the child reacts to events in his daily life: his reactions both in content and in form. As far as possible, we gather firsthand information about the daily occurrences in the child's life from persons in the immediate environment of the child, who are asked to provide us with all relevant details. In sifting their reports, we make due allowance for emotional relationships between our informants and the child. In addition, we ourselves invite the child to go on walks and outings, during which we try to attract his attention to various people who pass by, or we make him stop and look at show windows in order to discover what interests him; we visit public parks or playgrounds, and we let him watch other children at play, or induce him to take part in their games, etc.

In all these activities we learn about the child's reactions much more accurately than in the course of the most thorough and searching conversation.

### THE NARCISSISTIC TRANSFERENCE OF THE "JUVENILE IMPOSTOR"

Among the various types of wayward youth, one is striking because of the high degree of transference which is quickly developed. The relations to us of a youngster of this type remain through a long period of time so intensive and unmistakably positive, that we feel greatly encouraged in our capacity as counselors, and we continue our work with entire

confidence; indeed, we expect to see soon a full-fledged identification with us to develop from what had been so far
merely an object relationship. This would mean that a very
important phase of our pedagogic task is now completed. Yet
we experience each time the same unpleasant surprise; just
at this particular point, the young patient starts behaving not
at all as he should behave according to our own best judgment.
True, he does not relapse into his former misconduct; yet all
his manifestations show us distinctly, to our utter amazement,
that it is only now that the youngster begins to perceive us
as a separate object, and to recognize us as an independent
personality. This implies that he is still far from being able
to identify himself with us; because, in fact, during the entire
period of our previous work, he had failed to develop any
object-libidinal relationship to our person.

In its purest form, this type of juvenile delinquent is
represented by what we may call the "impostor" variety. It
was in such "mountebanks" that we first recognized a peculiar
psychic structure which makes them well-nigh incapable
of forming object-libidinal relations of any kind. The dependence upon ourselves, into which we succeeded to bring
them by purely intuitive means, must have been of an entirely
different nature. Nevertheless, with the help of a progressively more refined psychoanalytic insight, we managed somehow to understand our previous conduct (which was correct in
its own intuitive way) as well as the child's attitude to us,
and his behavior. Indeed, we progressed in our understanding until we finally became able consciously to provoke
those reactions required for successfully overcoming the
emotional distress.

The following case will give a fair idea of our method. A
mother, coming from a good middle-class milieu, visits our
child guidance clinic with her eighteen-year-old son; she complains that the young man has broken open her jewel box,
pilfered some jewels and pawned them. As the boy had never
been guilty of anything like this before, and as "it could not
be a case of bad upbringing" (according to his mother), the

only conclusion which the parents were able to reach was that it might have something to do with mental sickness. A doctor was therefore consulted. The doctor questioned the youth in detail, and learned that he needed a lot of money for his affairs with various girls: he had found no means of procuring it except by robbing his own mother. Thereupon the doctor insisted that the mother should bring her son to our child guidance clinic. We learn from the woman all relevant particulars about the family conditions, the childhood and the upbringing of the boy. After our conversation with the mother, we call in the young man.

This is the first impression he makes upon us: a youthful impostor who because of his peculiar psychic structure could not possibly have had those experiences with girls about which he boasted to the physician. Our attitude toward him is immediately, unambiguously determined by this first impression: we greet him with a handshake, in a matter-of-fact though not unfriendly way, without any words being spoken; and we motion him to take a seat.

"Why did you make fun of the doctor?" This is the question with which our talk begins.

"Because he asked for it," replies the boy, and he shrugs his shoulders.

"How much money do you have left?"

"One hundred and fifty shillings."

"Where do you keep them?"

"Here, in my pocket."

"Put the money on the table!" He obeys the order without any hesitation.

"Would you give this money back to your mother?"

"No!"

"But would you give it to me?"

"Yes, certainly."

I take an envelope, put the money in it, seal the envelope, write out a receipt for the sum of one hundred and fifty shillings, and hand this receipt over to the boy. While he takes it, I ask him:

"What are you thinking about, right now?"

"I think that it was silly of me to give you the money."

"Then why did you give it?"

"This I don't know."

"Try to think of a reason."

". . . Really, I don't know."

Without any transition, I start talking about school, and he tells me something of his life at home, while I just listen. After a few minutes, I interrupt him with the question:

"What are you thinking about now?"

"I cannot stop thinking how really stupid I was. Surely, I should not have given you that money."

"Then why did you give it? Ten minutes ago you did not even know me. Yet you gave it to me, and refused to give it back to your mother. I ask—why?"

"I don't know."

"Please think about it once more."

". . . Well, I have the feeling that you would have taken it out of my pocket anyhow. But now it is most annoying. I have promised two friends of mine to take them to the movies tonight, and now I have no money."

"Why don't you ask your mother to give you some?"

"That's out of the question. Now that she is so angry at me, I could not bring myself to ask her to pay the price of tickets to the movies."

"Don't you know any other way of getting some money?"

"No."

"Why can't you steal something again?"

"Are you joking?"

"I am not."

"But that's quite impossible!"

"Why not? Isn't there anything more that you might steal?"

"Well, in fact, there is. My sister's bracelet."

"Where is this bracelet?"

"In the drawer of the bedside table."

So now we start discussing this project of a theft in every detail, and I go even so far as to call his attention, at several points, to various ways of improving his method of stealing. This amazes him, but gradually his bad mood leaves him, when he sees a new possibility of getting money.

However, our conversation does not stop at that. The task of a child guidance worker can hardly consist in steering a juvenile delinquent toward actual thievery. So therefore I go on talking to him:

"All things considered, we shall not do it. We reserve the bracelet for such time when we might need more money. Meanwhile, may I ask you how much the tickets to the movie will cost?"

He mentions the figure, I take the sum out of my purse, and hand it to him. The young man is now completely disconcerted, for he has no idea where he stands with me. At first I had taken from him the remainder of his loot, then I had joined him on an imaginary expedition of robbery, and finally I give him the money he needs out of my own pocket.

I want to leave him for some time in this state of tension, and therefore I promptly send him away, while making another appointment with him for the next day.

On the next day, as soon as he enters our office, he makes the following cryptic remark:

"I must tell you something; or rather—no, I won't tell it to you."

I do not react, but only bid him to sit down. He takes a chair and starts again:

"Do you like Thomas Mann?"

"What have you read among the works of Thomas Mann?"

He mentions several titles, and goes on:

"We are now reading in class *Minna von Barnhelm* [he is in the last year of high school] and I cannot get through it." He indicates the passage they are studying, and expects me to comment upon it.

"Who wrote *Minna von Barnhelm?*"

"Lessing. Why do you look away from me at your books?"

At this point I feel the time has come to take more drastic action, and I ask:

"What are you driving at? Are you trying to prove me dumb?"

He is startled and exclaims:

"In your presence one is not even allowed to think for oneself."

"When you entered this room," I counter, "you wanted to tell me something; but then you forgot to tell me."

"That's true. It was about our cook. She told me to be careful with this man, he is a sly fox."

"Is she a shrewd person herself?"

"Not at all! She is quite stupid!"

"So how could she make such a remark?"

"Very simple: she was with us even before my birth, she likes me very much, and when mother found out about the theft, our cook sided with me wholeheartedly."

"And is your cook right as to the warning she gave you?"

"Oh, no, not at all!"

"Then tell me yourself [I now use the direct address, German second person *Du*] about your swindles which nobody has discovered as yet."

Thereupon, the youngster starts relating a long story of thievery, which goes back to when he was only ten years old. He had started with petty thefts at home, then he had pilfered costume jewelry and money from neighboring hotel rooms while traveling with his mother; or during summer vacations, from lockers in bathing establishments at the beach. There followed an uninterrupted series of misdeeds; his stealing became more ambitious in scope; and yet he was never caught at it, because nobody suspected "the well-bred boy from a respectable family."

These two interviews, just described, must now be considered from a psychoanalytic angle. Let us remember first of all what we have learned from Freud (1914) about an overflow of narcissistic libido.

Relations to the other person are not always of an object-libidinal nature. Under certain conditions there occurs a repression of object libido which is effective to a certain extent, with a corresponding setback of sensual impulses, and ultimately an overflow of narcissistic libido may result. Although the attitude toward the object becomes different in nature, this difference in the relationship is not recognized: the object is still perceived as if a libidinal object cathexis had actually taken place. Likewise, there is failure to recognize that this subject now serves the purpose of attaining the goals of one's own ego ideal. "One loves it for that perfection which should have crowned one's own ego, and which one tries now to reach by this round about way, for the satisfaction of one's narcissism" (Freud, 1914). If those desires that tend toward immediate sexual satisfaction are held back entirely, then the object keeps growing ever more grandiose, ever more valued. The object finally comes to take possession of the ego's entire self-love. Meanwhile, the functions which belong to the ego ideal are brought to a complete standstill. The critical faculty which is normally exercised by the ego ideal becomes silent; whatever is done or demanded by the person who serves as an object seems right and blameless. The voice of conscience is no longer heard in any occurrence where the outcome seems to favor the object. The entire situation may be summed up: the object has taken the place of the ego ideal.

How do we translate our theoretical insight into practical work? When we meet the type of juvenile delinquent described, then we do not attempt to establish an object-libidinal relationship at all. We behave from the beginning in a manner which incites the youngster to let his own narcissistic libido flow over to our person, so as ultimately to create that dependence of his total personality upon us, a situation parallel to the ego's dependency upon its ego ideal.

We follow this procedure because the practice of child guidance has taught us that for this type of wayward youth, there is no other way to reach a heightened degree of dependency relationship which we need in order to achieve our guidance task. We must take into consideration that any youngster who comes to the clinic finds himself in a psychic situation which is not the one we need: his attitude toward us is negative, often hostile; he feels uncertain, puzzled, irritated; he tries to show aloofness, or acts as if he were superior to us; sometimes he does not seem to be interested at all in what goes on. It is seldom that his posture is one of eager expectation.

One may think it important to establish from the outset, in each case, what is the patient's frame of mind, among these psychic states which we have just described. But we do not really need to know this because we can always provoke through our own behavior that labile state of tension required for our work.

A feeling of uncertainty must be induced in the patient at the first moment of meeting, by the very manner of our reception. Our way of receiving him is not always the same, for it depends entirely on the impression the youngster makes upon us. An example is given above, when we greeted the young man without uttering a word.

From the beginning, we put ourselves in the spotlight, we aroused the boy's interest in our person and awakened his desire to try his strength with us.

Hence our first question: "Why did you make fun of the doctor?" We asked this in order to resolve the labile situation in our favor. The content of the question informs the boy that we are wise to his tricks.

As to the specific shape and intonation of our sentence, it is designed to compel him to react as we wish. It is timed also to bring about the desired decision.

This part of our work may be described as the "timely use of the factor of surprise." While the juvenile delinquent is still unprepared for whatever awaits him and finds himself in a quite uncertain state of mind, there follows the dramatic act of unmasking, but without that dreaded consequence which is the only one he could have imagined: punishment.

He now observes that we are not the obnoxious adult who is called upon to castigate him; neither are we a teen-age comrade, prone to admire his courage or his smartness; in fact, we now seem to him a quite undecipherable being, of a species previously unknown, a person who indeed understands him, perhaps even with a slight undertone of appreciation, and who must be superior to him, in some inconceivable but not necessarily unpleasant manner. All this debate goes on not in his intellectual but in his emotional ego; for we do not move in his direction by way of verbal statements; it is only our general attitude which enables him to interpret our behavior, and after all he feels the interpretation might well be false. He is unable to reach a satisfactory conclusion, either in his own mind or through open discussion with the counselor; yet there remains the possibility to try to enter into a relationship with us—which he strives to attain for the benefit of his own ego, because he recognizes the "superiority" of our person. At this point, a careless observer might gain the false impression that an object-libidinal cathexis had actually taken place.

We take advantage of this situation immediately; we accept the privileged position being offered us, and we even strengthen it by asking about the money which was left over from the theft. We do so in a quiet, matter-of-fact manner, which excludes any contradiction.

In due time, there follows the question: "Would you give the money to me?" which is asked in order to find out whether the relation of dependency is already strong enough for active intervention on our part.

As to the receipt, we give it to him as a proof that the money remains his property, and that we consider him a fully responsible person; also, in order to avoid any suspicions he may entertain about our hidden intentions, such as the idea that we might hand the money back to his mother without his knowledge.

With the writing out of the receipt, the first phase of our work is completed. To proceed with our further task, we must find out what is his precise state of mind in the present moment. His answer to our question, "What are you thinking about, right now?" shows how necessary it was to establish that point.

The purpose of the conversation that ensues is to ascertain whether he still remains restless or whether he has become inwardly reconciled to the fact of not having the money any more. If we break off this talk so soon, and revert in our next questions to the previous theme, it is only because he evidently takes little interest in such topics as school and home, whereas his entire attitude shows plainly that he still thinks about the money which he has handed over.

"I have the feeling that you would have taken it out of my pocket anyhow"—this is an admission which seems to prove that his relationship to us has grown considerably closer, and that his dependence upon our person is now correspondingly stronger.

We learn, immediately thereafter, that he is greatly embarrassed at not having the money for buying movie tickets; and that he does not know how to procure this money. We refer him quite intentionally to his mother, on the obvious assumption that he will not dare ask her now for any favors. But this, in turn, must focus his attention on his own state of utter helplessness, while it makes us appear before his eyes as the unexpected savior, who without any prompting has brought him much-needed help.

Although the young man's relations to us have already reached a fairly high level of intensity, we are still far from being satisfied with the results. We want to take over more and more of his narcissistic libido, we intend to substitute ourselves for his ego ideal, so as to deprive him entirely of his critical faculty. In short, we plan to create a situation of dependency which would amount to nearly complete subservience.

Here a further observation is in order, for the benefit of

the child guidance worker. This maximum amount of relationship is necessary in the first phase of our work with this
specific kind of delinquent, inasmuch and in so far as we
treat him in our sole capacity as counselor; but such maximum can be reached only when the juvenile delinquent sees
in our person a superlative image of his own particular world.
He will not be able to follow what we prescribe for him, if
we are content to look upon his crime of stealing from the
mere standpoint of our social superego. It is not even enough
to show ourselves complacently tolerant in condoning his actions. Something more is required: we must "play the game
without restrictions," we must accept the boy's own values, we
must prove to him that we can live within his world, that we
ourselves represent a worth-while ideal by the standards of
this world—in other terms, that we are capable of stealing even more shrewdly than he.

We realize that all this puts us in a singularly dangerous
position, and we dare to do this only because we know that
it is this peculiar relationship with the wayward boy which
may stop him, perhaps, from committing another theft.

If we give him a little money, it is only in order to prevent
the necessity of some additional thievery. Moreover, our
generous act arouses in him such a storm of contradictory
feelings that he is overwhelmed and loses his bearings. We
do not allow him to come to any clear conclusions during
our first interview; we send him home regardless of whether
the "lesson" has come to an end; and we make a further
appointment with him.

Let us consider the second meeting. The remark which he
makes upon entering our office shows quite distinctly that
he is again mistrustful. Therefore, something must have occurred between yesterday and the present visit, something
of which we are still ignorant. Consequently, we remain
watchful, we do not press him to tell us what he does not
wish to tell, we avoid arousing his opposition; and so again
we invite him merely to take a seat.

But this time it is he who asks questions. He reverses
the situation of the previous day: yesterday we interrogated

him, now our turn has come to answer his queries. Of course we do not let ourselves be maneuvered; we counter his question with one of our own. Already after a few sentences, he abandons the pretence of talking about literature and reverts to the topic which brought us together. For he has noticed by now that we do not follow him, although he is still reluctant to give up his own line.

Our question, "What are you driving at? Are you trying to prove me dumb?" is the result of a parallel reasoning which was unfolding in our mind while the boy was putting his questions to us. We know that a juvenile delinquent of this type is extremely fond of displaying his smartness in front of everybody and on every conceivable occasion. He is very conceited about associating only with clever people.

The young man's demeanor and his questions make us aware that he wants to escape from the dependency which had been developed on the previous day. He tries to break out by luring us into a field, literature, where in his opinion we shall find ourselves at a disadvantage. Indeed, had we followed his leading questions, we would certainly have wasted our time, and perhaps given him an occasion to achieve his ends. But we did nothing of the sort. Through our own rejoinders, we made him understand that we were still his superior, as one the day before. The irrefutable proof that he finds himself in the same state of dependence lies in his manner of reacting to our question. He is startled, and he admits: "In your presence, one is not even allowed to think for oneself."

But if he is really enmeshed in a dependency relationship, then he must also have given up that feeling of distrust which was so noticeable at the moment of his coming. We want to watch our step and make quite sure of it, so as not to endanger the situation through any false move. Therefore we interject: "When you entered this room, you wanted to tell me something; but then you forgot to tell me." In order not to awaken again his mistrust, we put the stress on this word: "forgot."

The fight which we have to sustain against the cook is not

hard to win. Is she not a "stupid person?" We need only to put our questions in such a way as to remind our clever, "intellectual" young man of that fact.

Of course, we could not have guessed in advance that this "silly" old woman, the cook, would enable us to get the boy's almost full confession as early as our second interview, a confession involving nearly all the thefts of which the delinquent was still consciously aware. Nor could we have foreseen that it would suffice, in these circumstances, to use the direct, familiar address (German second person *Du*) in order to clinch a highly strengthened web of relationship to our person.

To create an element of surprise in order to startle the patient is not, however, an easy task. One cannot prepare oneself in advance; the surprise should result from circumstances that are by their very nature instantaneous; and each situation must be absolutely mastered as soon as it arises. A correct estimate of actions and consequences, even before they are set in motion, as well as a capacity for swift combination and immediate decision, are the prerequisites for achieving those dramatic effects which will work out as factors of surprise.

Here is an example. A youngster, who had received a suspended sentence for theft, was kept for a very long time under welfare observation. One day, the social worker, a woman, brings the young man to our child guidance clinic, because she has been suspecting him for some time of manifest homosexual practices.

This social worker has had considerable experience. She treats her charge in accordance with the situation. In her eyes he is a grownup, and she tries to influence him favorably by her own straightforwardness because she has discovered certain elements in his character which should readily respond to such treatment.

From her reports of the youngster's present conduct, it appears that she takes care even of his pocket-money needs, providing him each week with petty cash and receiving his expense accounts, which she checks with the boy against his personal daily records, a procedure that was started on her initiative. She is particularly happy that the boy writes down even superfluous and unjustified expenses which must mean that he has nothing to hide from his counselor.

The reception of this boy at our clinic turns out to be rather unusual: the social worker introduces us to each other as if we were at a society meeting. His attitude is not that of the juvenile delinquent who presents himself before a child guidance counselor; in fact, he behaves as if he were a superior person whom his friend, the social worker, had invited to see me, because I showed interest in him. Obviously, he does not know that this "invitation" was merely a pretense, to make sure that he would come.

Right after the introduction, the social worker excuses herself and is about to go, so as to leave me alone with the boy. But just before going, she takes him to a corner of the office. I do not know what they are talking about, but I can see that he is receiving some money from her, and that his lips twitch momentarily in a half-smile of disparagement, only to resume at once its friendly, noncommittal expression. The social worker, busy with her purse, does not notice anything.

When we are alone, I ask him immediately about his talk with the social worker and I ask it in a way as to make him aware that I have marked his smile. He retorts by asserting that she had merely asked whether he needed money for the trolley car, and then had given him the money. Moreover, he goes on to say, the social worker had settled his accounts with him only the day before, and she knew therefore that he was out of money. I am not impressed by this remark, and I demand instead that he show me his purse—a demand which I make in a tone that admits no contradiction. He seems completely taken aback, produces the purse at once, hands it over to me after a moment of hesitation, and waits in utter embarrassment. In the purse I find about twenty shillings in silver and banknotes, as well as a slip of paper on which are marked the names and addresses of two men, with corresponding appointments. Without further examination, I reproach him bluntly with his manifestly homosexual practices, for which he even gets paid. He is so surprised at being found out that he does not try to deny the facts, and admits everything. Later, however, in the course of the conversation, he regains some of his self-assurance, and his statements again become mendacious.

How clever this young man is in misleading people can be seen from the following remark, made in answer to my question as to why he was lying so brazenly to the social worker: "When, in checking my accounts with her, I show her that I have no money, she thinks that I must be a decent guy, she makes favorable reports to the authorities, and I am left alone to do as I please."

Another example is a young man of twenty-two, who has been driven from home by his own family, because of repeated swindles and thefts, and sent away to live with some relatives abroad. But now they are complaining that the young man is guilty of new acts of swindling. Upon receipt of this additional information, the parents, in complete despair, decide to visit our clinic.

The counselor explains to the parents that he cannot take any steps without interviewing the young man personally; whereupon they arrange for his return. Meanwhile, there appears at the clinic a friend of the family who on behalf of the parents asks for instructions as to how they should behave upon their son's arrival. But the counselor, relying on what he knows of the mutual relationship between members of this family, deems it important to meet the young man himself, before his reunion with his parents. He therefore suggests that the family friend should go to the railway station instead of the parents, and that he should bring Franz directly to me. The suggestion is accepted and carried out. Franz remains in the waiting room at the clinic while the friend goes into my office and tells me the following news: "You cannot imagine how Franz behaves! His aloofness is indescribable,

I cannot stand his demeanor of icy coldness, he has not spoken one word since I met him at the station."

Intentionally, I leave Franz alone for a full hour in the waiting room. Meanwhile, the family friend relates further information about the young man and his parents. My line of reasoning is this: should this remarkable behavior of my young patient prove to be only a "mask," then he will not be able to bear to bear his solitude, in an alien environment, not knowing what will happen next; therefore he will break down and become more accessible. On the other hand, if his haughtiness happens to be genuine, it will certainly end in an emotional outburst, after such a long wait which he will interpret as neglect of his person and regard as an outrage. As to other possibilities, such as listening at the door out of sheer curiosity, or remaining uninterested and aloof, I could rule them out, because of all I had learned about the character of Franz.

At the end of this "hour of waiting," I open the door which leads to the anteroom, in order to show Franz into my office. He is no longer the same Franz, but a bundle of wretchedness, a young man who has lost every semblance of self-control, and who now cowers miserably in a corner.

I take him by the hand, I address him without transition in the direct second person [German *Du*], I lead him into my office with these few words: "Don't be ashamed, let yourself cry as much as you wish!" Franz dissolves in a stream of tears, and it takes some time to pull himself together. He starts telling me, still sobbing, the pitiful story of his life: about himself, his parents who never understood him, the circumstances at home and in school, and a childhood without joy. This first interview is enough to unfold the sad picture of a really unhappy child.

The transference is achieved immediately, and holds fast for the duration of the treatment.

One more example: An estate manager from abroad comes to our clinic for consultation, and brings his son, who is considered in his family as a swindler. Father and son walk together into my office; because of the peculiar attitude of the son I lack the opportunity of having a preliminary talk with the father alone. The demeanor of this young man, who seems to be around twenty-five, shows that he has no use for the entire procedure; he glances at us inquiringly, but with the most supercilious expression, as if to convey the idea that there is no point in our present meeting.

The father recounts at great length the offenses committed by his son, whose behavior displays only a growing boredom. The statements of the father concern him as little as if they were made about someone else. Obviously, he has only one desire: that this annoying conversation should come to a stop.

When the father finishes his report, I reply in a tone which, at first, seems to ignore the son's presence altogether: "I do not treat cases of swindling; it would be a pity to waste my time and your money; if your son commits no further offense, everything will be all right anyhow; and should he revert to his old tricks, then they will lock him up, and you shall be rid of him." Turning to the son, I then continue: "Or perhaps you prefer to shoot yourself, if you are not a coward. This is another way of closing the case." While I speak these words calmly, without emotion, in a tone which I keep intentionally on the level of a matter-of-fact observation, I stand up in order to show that the interview has come to an end.

The father looks nonplussed and utterly dismayed. But from the countenance of the son one may note that we have succeeded in causing that state of irritation we intended to provoke. At the exit door, I shake hands with the young man, and add these few words: "You shall find no treatment at my clinic, but if you wish to talk with me once more, you may come and see me tomorrow." I also indicate the exact time at which I shall be expecting him.

After a short while, the father returns alone and starts complaining bitterly about my unbelievable behavior, which he fails to understand. Of course my purpose, in behaving as

I did, escaped him entirely. So I explain to him the necessity of my line of conduct, which was dictated by the attitude taken by the son. I insist that he must not in any way influence his son's decision whether he should visit me again. Finally, the father goes away with a much easier mind.

On the next day, at the appointed hour, the young man comes to my office in a quite different mood—he is much less tense, more open to argument, and full of expectation: the transference has begun to work.

### Concluding Remarks

In the course of this paper, we have met with a series of concrete instances wherein the reader might easily have gained the impression that success in child guidance work hinges above all upon the personality of the child guidance worker: a person friendly to other human beings, ready to help his fellows, able to make decisions, capable through his unerring intuition to feel his way among the emotions and relationships of strangers. The worker would exert great influence upon both parents and children, and without giving it much thought would bring about a transference, so to speak automatically, as a spontaneous result of his entire being. Conversely, the person who locks himself up in his own thoughts, his own feelings and intentions, or who hesitates to reach any decision out of an exaggerated conscientiousness, and cannot break through the barrier of a relationship between strangers because he is too considerate to hurt the feelings of other people—such a person would be unsuited for the calling of a child guidance counselor. Even with readiness to help, he would not achieve anything, as the clients who seek his guidance would not be instinctively convinced by his advice.

If such considerations were valid, it would necessarily follow that there exists only one factor which is paramount in the training of child guidance workers: namely, the selection of those persons who happen to be suited by their very nature for such a career.

All this is true in the case of that category of counselors who lack psychoanalytic education, and who must therefore rely upon the resources of their own personality to gain whatever successful results they chance to achieve.

However, our work at the child guidance clinic rests upon different foundations. Although no counselor will ever consider that the gift of intuition is superfluous, his knowledge of the human being whom he treats derives nevertheless from another source: from the result of those inquiries which the science of psychoanalysis has conducted into the development of the ego and of man's instinctual life.

But the method of psychoanalysis has given us more than that: it is the discoveries made in the process of psychoanalytic work, concerning the resolution of neurotic conflicts, which provide us with understanding, with opportunities for further study and promise of successful therapy in the broad field described by the over-all term of delinquency.

Formerly, the educator and child guidance worker stood helpless in front of an indescribable chaos of faulty development in children; all too often, he was tempted to concur in the verdict which society and the courts pronounced against the juvenile delinquent. Whereas today, when he makes good use of the insights and systematic results of psychoanalysis, the counselor finds himself at last in a position to build up gradually a symptomatology, etiology, and therapy for the various phenomena of delinquency; and he may even hope for some ultimate cure of delinquency. Society and the state should no longer rest content with a one-sided prosecution of wayward youth as a measure of self-protection, when preventive and curative methods are already close at hand. But let us remember that without the lifelong efforts of Sigmund Freud, there would be no such bright prospects for the future betterment of these severely handicapped young people.

# VI

## The Education of the Unsocial

The ultimate aim of child rearing is, in theory, the attainment of that ideally social condition in which each individual lives with the least disturbance according to his own personality, while still fulfilling obligations necessary in the life of any social community. As a social being, man confronts a collectivity not only as an ego; he belongs to it also as one of its individuals. Therefore he has to satisfy two different sets of conditions: the one in respect to society, and the other in respect to himself. Child rearing should always let the person develop in such a way that his experiences and way of life harm neither himself nor the society in which he lives. Even if the social ideal itself is liable to change, this does not modify the fundamental goal. Psychoanalysis has defined its educational aims in the following way: every well-brought-up person should be able to solve, in accordance both with his ego and with the claims of reality, those conflicts which originate from the fulfillment or frustration of his various needs.

The individual is not social when he fails to meet the requirements of a collectivity, and also when he neglects the

"Die Erziehung Unsozialer." In: *Das psychoanalytische Volksbuch*, ed. P. Federn and H. Meng. Bern: Huber, 1939, pp. 290-315.

requirements of his own personality. Conversely, it is the collectivity which behaves unsocially when it tries to protect itself from the individual while failing to protect the individual from society.

We are in the habit of describing as delinquent any acts which are directed against the community, and we clearly distinguish delinquency from neurosis. Yet both types of behavior are antisocial. Both are the effects of a defensive tendency. When there occurs in childhood a conflict between the individual and the social needs, the child may protect himself against such conflict situations in one of two opposite ways. The conflict will be fought through in delinquency by antagonizing the outside world; or, if the balance of forces does not allow such provocation, the conflict will develop inwardly, as a neurosis. With different symptoms and in contrary directions, we have the same phenomenon: developing inwardly with a deficiency of instinctual expression; or outwardly with an excess of expression.

These manifestations are so manifold that it is worth while, even at this stage, to attempt some definition of concepts, which would eventually make possible a more systematic comprehension of the problem.

Early training guides the development of the child according to certain definite values. The little child is at first below any standards of upbringing: he is asocial. Educators, whoever they happen to be, know that this condition is normal until a certain age in childhood. When the influences of rearing remain ineffectual even after this age is reached, the educator's attitude changes. What was previously considered normal must now be treated as abnormal. The uneducable[1] child accordingly remains asocial, while the educable child outgrows this condition by gradual stages: the one is absolutely asocial, the other relatively asocial. If we examine the causes of uneducability, we are led to a further subdivision

---

[1] *Editor's Note:* Aichhorn means here the child who does not respond to parental training in the usual sense. "Uneducable" *(unerziehbar)* might also be translated as untrainable or incorrigible.

of the absolutely asocial: they may be subdivided, for instance, according to whether the main cause of the disability lies in one of the intellectual functions (understanding, attention, memory, etc.), or in affectivity, or in some organic disease, or in a psychic trauma.

The relatively asocial children can be guided toward a normal development in the sense of the social ideal, provided their psychic structure has not been disturbed, notably in respect to the distribution of libido, and provided that the persons who rear them are themselves socially minded. If a child is brought up in an environment where the orientation happens to be entirely asocial, as for example in a family of criminals, then he may become asocial through unavoidable identification with the persons who bring him up even if his development remains otherwise normal. Nevertheless, such a child must be classified among the relatively asocial, if his constitutional disposition would make him educable in more favorable circumstances. We would like to define this group as "pseudo-asocial." But if there is no one with whom the child might identify himself—e.g., the case of Tarzan—or if the environment shifts so frequently—as happens with wards of welfare agencies—that the child would lack the time to develop object cathexes (i.e., love for somebody) and identification (the taking of somebody's example), then this state might well become permanent. These few remarks suffice to indicate a further subdivision within the group of the relatively asocial.

The emotional ties between the members of a family create the atmosphere in which the child grows up. If the relationship within the family leads to a state of libidinal equilibrium, then the child escapes the dangers which might otherwise threaten him because of the emotional outbursts of the adults. If this equilibrium is upheld only through artificial means, by a too exclusive concentration of one of the parents upon the child; of if the equilibrium is destroyed because there is not enough libido available, then one may expect far-reaching disturbances in the child's development.

One of the two parents always tends unconsciously to over-burden the child, in a libidinal sense, when the other parent fails to satisfy the libidinal needs of his mate. A meaningful formulation would be the following: whenever one of the parents tries to keep down the symptoms of his own neurosis, the state of libidinal equilibrium within the family, the intrafamilial libido constellation, will be upheld at the cost of the child.

This makes the child at first heistant, then more and more irritable, in his emotional ties with his surroundings, until his libidinal economy suffers such an upset that an abnormal relationship arises. Henceforward, the child's up-bringing becomes a failure and the result is an asocial child. The earlier this stage is reached in childhood, the more infantile, the more untrained the child remains, because of this inhibition in development. The later it sets in, the fur-ther the child progresses. He will not remain static at this stage, but will revert through a process of regression, as experience teaches us time and again, to an earlier infantile condition.

In both cases—of developmental inhibition and of regres-sion—it can happen that the behavior such children will apparently coincide in content as well as in form with those observable in asocial children. But these expressions have a different motivation, and a keen observer will have no trouble in perceiving them as "different." In the one type of behavior, *the norms are not yet understood* by the child; in the other type, the child *has no longer the ability to understand rules.* On the other hand, we observe manifestations which have nothing to do with the libidinal relationship between the child and educators (parents); on the other, we deal with disturbed libidinal relations. If we note the unsocial expres-sions of such children, we gain the impression that they serve a definite unconscious purpose. The children attempt to satisfy unconsciously all kinds of libidinal strivings, but they try to do so with worthless means. In contradistinction to the asocial type, these children may be grouped together as "dissocial."[2] This group would comprise the many types of juvenile delinquents and neurotics.

So far, very little interest has been shown in discovering the motives of this kind of behavior. One is content, in most cases, to accept the facts at their face value, and to master the problems of delinquency and of incorrigibility by taking recourse to the well-tried but insufficient means of routine. Every reader knows the delinquent child from daily experience, from newspaper reports about police and trial proceedings. He also knows the near-uneducable child, the boy who causes trouble in school, who is unruly at home, who disturbs order and harmony everywhere, makes life miserable for his teacher, and drives his parents to despair—until no one knows how to handle him.

The youth welfare worker often finds himself in a position where he must express his opinion about a child who is almost untrainable; and not seldom he gets the following answer: "Near-uneducability? This is only a catchword. Let us forget all this sentimental nonsense, and let us restore the old principle of authority in the upbringing of children, such as we ourselves experienced. We shall then put an end not only to the so-called uneducability, but also to the entire problem of delinquency." But those parents who apply to us in dire need speak an altogether different language: "We have treated our child with severity, we have disciplined and punished him, and we have achieved nothing. We have also tried mildness and kindness, but this too has brought no results. What shall we do now?"

Well, who is right? Those people who consider it absurd to build up a training on the psychological study of the child, or those parents who ask us for some pedagogic means other than the usual routine of upbringing?

Some time ago, I had an appointment with one of my friends. When I reached the door of his apartment, I heard an awful tumult: the shrill outcries of a boy, interrupted by

[2] *Editor's Note:* Aichhorn's term is *"dissozial,"* difficult to translate. "Unsocial" seems too mild for his meaning.

the irate voice of my friend and intermingled with exclamations by an excited woman, all this accompanied by noise characteristic of corporal punishment.

I go in!—My friend has laid his ten-year-old son, Kurt, across his knee and is flogging him. The wife runs to me in a state of wild agitation and bursts out: "The lad has not deserved such flogging! My husband must stop beating him immediately!"

The father not only stops, but pushes Kurt toward me and adds with a sneer: "He is all yours. You may try your educational skills on this good-for-nothing son of mine!" I understand his glance and ironical words; he has no high opinion of our brand of training.

"But for Heaven's sake, tell me at least what's it all about?"

From the account of the excited parents, who were interrupting and trying to correct each other, it was not difficult to piece together the cause of this ugly scene. The father had wanted to teach Kurt the elements of arithmetic, because the school reports were invariably bad and his mother's efforts had so far proved to be unsuccessful. But even with his father, Kurt's arithmetic did not improve. The father became more and more impatient, he started to ask questions in a sharper tone, failing to notice that this served only to intimidate and frighten the boy, whose answers were now all wrong. Growing increasingly angry, my friend called him names: lazy, stupid, inattentive, scatterbrained, and then started giving him one slap after another. Meanwhile, in the next room, his wife was following this crescendo of conflict between father and son, until finally she could no longer control herself. She upbraided her husband indignantly for the unseemly way in which he treated the child. My friend, incensed at this intervention and utterly disgusted at having begotten such a stupid boy, answered back sharply. It all ended in a violent quarrel between the parents in the presence of the child; the boy, more and more emboldened, started openly to side with his mother and to complain about the father's injustice. The final catastrophe had occurred just before my arrival. The father, unable to cope with the combined attack of mother and child, had flown into a senseless rage, seized the rod, and proceeded to try to teach Kurt better behavior.

It was some time before the parents became amenable to a sensible exchange of views, and it took even longer before they calmed down to the point where they recognized the inadmissibility of such a scene with the child, or in his presence. I declared myself ready to help Kurt with his arithmetic; not right now, when the nervous boy was still quite upset, but some other day.

This is what happened one week later: Kurt sits with me and we go over the rudiments of multiplication. The boy's counting is exceedingly bad, yet the most remarkable feature is the recurrence of the figure *eight* in the child's wrong answers: $5 \times 7 = 38, 9 \times 6 = 58, 8 \times 8 = 68, 5 \times 9 = 48$. Occasionally, a few replies happen to be right. But when I ask, "How much is $3 \times 6$?" I get no answer at all, although the boy took some time to think it over. So far, I had not tried to correct the erroneous results, and I did not tell the child that three times six was eighteen. Now I stop counting and ask Kurt if he has noticed that most of his replies are wrong. He seems surprised and claims that it is not so. I go over it again: "You have said $5 \times 7 = 38$, instead of 35; $9 \times 6 = 58$, instead of 54; $8 \times 8 = 68$, instead of 64; and so forth." While talking, I write down the figures 38, 58, 68, 48, etc., and let him read them. But Kurt fails to notice the repeated 8. I now draw his attention to this fact. "Not only have you multiplied incorrectly, but each time you have brought back this figure 8." After reading his results once more, he recognizes the correctness of my statement and shows great surprise.

The following conversation now takes place between us:

"Where does this 8 come from?"

"I really don't know."

"Try to imagine this 8!"

"I can't do it."

"Close your eyes and try again."

"Now I see an 8."

"What kind of 8?"

"The 8 on the streetcar 18." (He means the number on the front of Line No. 18 of the Vienna electric streetcars.)

"Did anything happen to you on a car of Line 18?"

"Yes!"

"What exactly?"

"We had an outing with the school, and there was a boy who got his finger squeezed in the door of the streetcar; it was bleeding horribly."

"Did anything else ever happen on Line 18?"

"No, nothing at all. But my teacher gave me a map of Vienna; the electric railways are marked in red, and I like it very much."

"Do you have such a liking for the color red?"

"I like blue better."

"Try to imagine this blue color."

"I can't, all I see now is red."

"When I think of a color, I see it at once on some definite object; what is the thing which *you* see as red?"

"I see a press with two rollers, and there is red paper coming out of it all the time."

"Look well at this red paper, and tell me more about it!"

The boy remained silent for a while, and although he keeps his eyes shut, one can see by his features how deeply absorbed he is in the imaginary picture. His expression shows growing surprise, he opens his eyes and says: "This is not red paper at all, this is blood, flowing from the wounds of the dragon that Siegfried killed!"

This statement remains incomprehensible until we learn that Kurt has gone to a movie the day before and seen a picture of the Nibelungen saga. Then we begin to suspect that the child has become overexcited at the movies, that he has not yet overcome the emotion he experienced there. He has certainly nothing against Siegfried's killing the dragon, but the stream of gore must have been very distasteful to this sensitive boy. It "gave him the creeps," as he explained to me.

What has all this to do with Kurt's poor performance in arithmetic? This is indeed something which we do not yet know. Let us leave it uninvestigated for the time being. Let us wait until the child himself provides us with more information. All we need to assume at this stage is that the excitement of the day before is still active, and that it must be removed before we can make further progress.

I draw Kurt's attention to the fact that the dragon is not a living animal but a cardboard contraption, and I explain to him rather circumstantially how such moving pictures are made. He listens with great interest and feels visibly better after my explanation. Somewhat later, I tell him: "Isn't it amusing that after counting wrongly you happened to have in mind a streetcar of Line 18, then a bleeding finger, then the red lines on the map, then the red paper coming from the press, and finally the blood of the dragon?" Thereupon the boy adds: "I remember something else. When we were on vacation in F., I saw a bicycle rider fall; he bashed his head and was bleeding, and his front wheel made an eight." (When the wheel of a vehicle is all bent after a fall or a crash, we used to say that it "makes an eight.")

Doubtless, there exist for Kurt certain intimate and unusual associations between "blood" and the figure "eight"; and these relations reappear in connection with the number 18 on the streetcar. It is certainly not without interest to examine a little more closely the links which brings this about.

We constantly receive impressions from our environment, and they are often unpleasant. When these are accompanied by strong emotion we speak of *affective* experiences. But it frequently occurs that the unpleasant affect, which according to its origin should be connected only with some definite impression, becomes associated with other impressions received at the same time, which from then on slumber in our minds as unpleasant, without our knowing why it is so.

In the case of Kurt, we may imagine the process in approximately the following way. The fall of the bicycle rider induces in the boy a state of extraordinary excitement. But the affect which he thus experiences becomes associated not only with the image of the rider's bleeding head but also, without the child's knowledge, with the contemporaneously developing notion about the *eight*like shape of the crumpled wheel and the figure *eight* more generally. The link becomes even stronger when a schoolmate has a finger squashed on a streetcar of Line 18.

In order to understand Kurt's behavior, we must know that not all the impressions received in the course of an experience are necessarily remembered at the moment we try to bring the incident back to mind. In most cases, only a few images emerge, to the exclusion of the others, which are repressed and remain forgotten.

Kurt is so disturbed by the dragon's blood that he cannot get rid of the memory. Although he is no longer conscious of this strong feeling, it is still present somewhere in his mind. When the boy makes errors in counting and when his results keep showing the figure eight, this figure stands really for "blood" and penetrates the boy's consciousness: the disturbance is caused by the affective pressure which seeks discharge. We have seen how I proceeded in order to relieve the affect, and how Kurt seemed to breathe more freely after he had recognized the connections. Of course I had merely scratched the surface of the phenomena without penetrating deep into the psyche of the boy. But the experiment was instructive. If it had proved possible to remove an affect which was dominant the day before, then one could also discover further connections. This I did in the following way.

I let the boy shut his eyes once more and asked him to call again to his mind the figure eight.

He did not succeed at first. He opened the eyes and said: "Whenever I enter a streetcar of Line 18, I have such an unpleasant feeling. . . ."

"Do you feel the same thing on cars of any other line?"
"No!"

"Now try to represent to yourself the figure eighteen."

He shuts his eyes: "I see it now on a plate which looks like the number plate of a house."

"What house could that be?"

"It is our school building."

"Why is it your school?"

"This I don't know."

"Open your eyes! Try to think and find out why it is that a house number 18 reminds you of your own school!"

For a while he cannot discover any connection; but it developed that "going to school" had seemed to him somewhat frightening, and that even in his free time he was reluctant to go anywhere near his school. Now he also remembers that the unpleasant feeling in entering a streetcar of Line 18 is exactly the same feeling as that he experiences in approaching the school. In the middle of the talk he interrupts himself to reflect: "Now I know why I could not tell how much three times six is!"

"Why?"

"Three times six is eighteen, which is also Line 18, and number 18 on the building of our school."

This recollection, which formerly was not admitted into the conscious mind, happens to be correct: the house number of Kurt's school is in fact 18.

After this conversation, which had disclosed only superficial connections, we resumed our exercises in arithmetic and from now on Kurt counted without any errors. The parents, the teacher, but most of all Kurt himself were very much surprised; for, since that memorable day, he had no more trouble with multiplication.

The way in which Kurt had been handled did not amount to a psychoanalytic treatment. It was only an attempt to talk things over with the boy, to help him overcome his concrete difficulties by uncovering certain connections which lay near the surface of his mind, though they had already become unconscious. The success of such a talk should not be overestimated. The severely neurotic reaction of this child must have had deeper causes, which remained hidden from us.

Nor does this isolated result afford any general conclusions about inhibitions in arithmetic among schoolchildren. Such inhibitions are not always connected with the house number of the school. In most instances, only psychoanalytic treatment can provide the remedy. Nevertheless, we may learn, even from this one case, something of importance for parents and teachers.

Bad performance at school is not always the result of a child's poor capacity. It is quite possible that substandard performance originates in emotional disorders.

Difficulties in learning capacity and in educability, if they have developed on a neurotic basis, cannot be overcome either through patience or through mildness and kindness; and even less so, by severity and punishment. As long as one cannot render conscious those connections which the child has repressed with their affective content, any attempt will remain unsuccessful.

We now have an idea of how a child seeks to overcome a definite anxiety situation, and herewith we have touched upon a problem that has received very little attention. It is not only the repressed, yet still active anxiety affect which may torment the child. It happens often that the child withdraws his interest from the outer world and devotes it entirely to fantasies, which will then emerge as daydreams. An exceedingly large number of children yield willingly to pleasurable imaginings, or, on the contrary, are plagued against their will by frightful phantasms and terrifying visions. They are often unable to ward off their daydreams even while sitting in the classroom, and they do not follow their lessons at school. Yet a teacher would be wrong in judging these daydreamers as guilty merely of inattention and absent-mindedness. He is probably inclined to think that such pupils would achieve more if only they were less inattentive and tried to concentrate on their lessons. But the poor scholastic performance of these inherently clever children is due not to their absent-mindedness, or to any unwillingness to learn. On the contrary, these children are already too much absorbed, not in the teacher's lessons, but in their own fantasies. Certainly, they could achieve more —though not if they so wished, but if they were free to wish it. Most educators (both teachers and parents) fail to inquire into the causes of such striking inhibition in a child's ability to study; and this oversight is not without influence on the child's reaction. He feels he is treated unjustly, and he responds by taking up an attitude of defense. This is misconstrued as stubbornness, obduracy, defiance, and is treated with severity. The child who is easy to irritate takes on a still more defensive position and this stirs up the emotions of his educators to greater intensity. Both sides, the child and the parents, the pupil and the educator, the schoolboy and the schoolteacher, irritate each other more and more. What was formerly a series of isolated incidents becomes a permanent situation. Parents and teachers are now confronted with a child whom they regard as nearly uneducable; his behavior leaves them puzzled and helpless.

There are many other forms of near-uneducability motivated in different ways, but all of them grow out of a basically neurotic condition. One further remark is important: though the development of these children shows a deviation from the norm, they should not be described as "sick" children. What they need is attentive care and a psychoanalytically orientated education. In exceptionally difficult cases, they would require psychoanalytic treatment.

At this point we may add a few general remarks concerning normality and abnormality in child development.

Descended from a given line of ancestors, the child comes into the world with a definite hereditary predisposition, which forms his constitution. Were each child to behave in life in an individual manner—that is, in strictest accordance with his native disposition—then he would become anything but a social being. Indeed, in every collectivity, entirely individual behavior displayed by each member would encounter the obstacle of a similar tendency on the part of all other members; and this would render impossible any social community. Within human society, the one who does not give up, under pressure of all his fellows, that part of his individuality which hinders the possibility of living together will exclude himself from the community and must ultimately perish, if (as is usually the case) he happens to be the weaker party. Therefore, society cannot remain indifferent to the manner in which children develop. Society is forced to influence the growing generation according to definite patterns, and cannot pay much attention to the individual needs of its members for unique ways of life. What is important for society is only the end result: man as a social being. This is why we all know what the demands of organized society upon the maturing youth are, while we know little about the child himself, beyond what is needed to satisfy his most elementary wants. Society has set up certain standards as to how one should rear, guide, and educate children. Yet we are hardly conscious of the fact that rearing consists in a one-sided pressure exercised upon the child, so as to induce him to relinquish some part of his own individuality. He must give up all those cravings which would make collective life difficult or impossible. Whatever we do in this respect, the child will always resent it as an act of violence, and he will naturally react by taking up a defensive position. Yet the facts of the case remain quite unknown to most parents. They live on, giving vent to their emotions, unconcerned with those of the child, and are taken aback only when the child's upbringing brings a different result from the one expected. Some parents who are informed about these phenomena in the life of children take certain precautions. But the more radical reformers go to the other extreme. They are convinced that a child should live according to his own nature, expressing his pent-up emotions, and that he will be healthy only if allowed to do whatever he pleases. These reformers overlook the fact that in such an upbringing the grownups become mere observers of the manifestations of juvenile vitality. Any real training means perforce the setting up of certain demands which restrict the child's instincts; it also means having the power of enforcing these demands. Whether this goal can be achieved through mildness and kindness, that is, through the premium of love, or through severity, by threats and punishment, is another question. What is open to discussion is not the *aim* of education but the *means*. It is a matter of course that children will try to put up a defense against the pressures of rearing. An upbringing without restrictions and inhibitions produces people who cannot live in a social community. Once we have recognized these hard facts, we shall gain an understanding of many expressions of child life, and interpret them as defensive reactions. We shall then find it easier to discover the right path among the many obstacles which beset the educator and parent.

Within the family, from earliest babyhood, the parents are the exacting representatives of society. In most cases, it is the father who restricts and deflects the instinctual urges. He does not allow everything which the child wants; his mere presence may often suffice to inhibit the wishful impulses. But the parents are not solely persons who refuse; they are also wish-fulfilling persons. The child gains a special feeling of affection for his parents and develops object-libidinal relations with them.

As Freud has demonstrated, such object relationships acquire a particular significance in the development of the child's "ego." The demands of the father (or the mother) become incorporated in the ego of the child, due to a very complicated psychic process known in psychoanalysis as "identification." Whatever the parents have succeeded in imposing upon the child as commandments and prohibitions is transmitted to the ego of the maturing youth. There it plays the part of a severe judge and watchman, always vigilant and ready to criticize the so-called superego.

This explains why the personality of the educators is of decisive importance. It is easy to understand that a social activity is possible only when the individual has a socially directed superego, one he is ready to follow willingly. Unsocial behavior occurs when the superego shows defects and deficiencies; that is, when it possesses such features as are incompatible with society's requirements; or when the superego, though orientated in a social way, fails to overcome an ego which refused obedience.

We can understand various types of delinquency by assuming that the superego is deficient, or not severe enough in its demands. On the other hand, an excessively demanding superego may lead to neurotic disease, or, given certain preconditions, to near-uneducability. The parents themselves acquired a rigid set of attitudes in their own childhood days, and it is these attitudes which in turn regulate, often quite unconsciously, the parental behavior toward the child, down to the smallest detail. Much of the behavior of children we understand only after we have gathered sufficient information about the childhood of the parents. A child's behavior is only so many reactions to the doings of his parents or other persons of his environment.

A good example follows. One day, there appears a very nice woman of the working class, about thirty-six years old. She needs my help, she is bewildered and desperate. Her twelve-year-old boy undoubtedly must be committed to a correctional institution, because he behaves so terribly that only the severest discipline may perhaps—in *her* opinion— lead him to better ways. After her outbreak of despair, I ask the mother a simple question: "What are the awful things he has done?" The reply: "He is disobedient, insolent, obstinate, and so corrupt that he even tripped his own father. But this is not all, oh no! A week ago, he failed to get the signature on the register from the competent welfare official, so that I did not receive any allowance for the last term. He knows how badly we need the money; he did this to me quite purposely; he is really a heartless lad, who loves nobody; I don't want to see him any more." I let the mother pour out all this, and many other things besides; I allow her to unburden herself without interrupting her story, whether her words seem important or irrelevant to me, because I want her first of all to get rid of her affect, and because I hope to discover in this torrent of complaints some significant details.

From her account one can piece together the picture of a neatly ordered, if materially unprosperous family life. Her husband, who is at present unemployed and has no income but his social security allowance, loves her and shows affection for the child; he helps him with his schoolwork, he spends much time and plays games with him, in a manner which is not common among people of his class. The man does not play cards and does not drink, and he devotes his life entirely to his wife and child. Our welfare worker confirms the story. The woman herself looks trustworthy. The school has no particular complaints against the boy. He is studious and is well liked by his schoolmates. On the other hand, he is lively and uncontrolled, and shows great reluctance to accept school discipline. After all that I had heard about this family, the behavior of the boy seemed difficult to understand. I therefore asked the mother for additional details.

"Did Franz always behave that way?"

"He has always been a wild boy, but never as bad as during the last six weeks."

"Do you know any reason for this remarkable deterioration in his behavior?"

"No, nothing."

"Does Franz sleep in the same room with you and your husband?"

"Yes, he sleeps on a couch. Previously, he slept at my side, in one of the twin beds."

"Since when does he use the couch?"

"About a year and a half ago."

"Why did you transfer him to the couch?"

"Because my companion came then to live with us."

"You are not married?"

"No, my husband was killed in the war."

"When was he drafted?"

"In August 1914, and from that time we never saw him again."

"Have you remained single since then, or did you live with anyone else?"

"Until Easter last year I lived all alone with Franz."

"Didn't you have great difficulties with your child?"

"Not at all, he behaved quite well."

"Did he change when your companion started living with you?"

"Not particularly; anyhow he likes him too, very much."

"But didn't you tell me previously that the boy has always been quite unrestrained?"

"Well, yes, naturally, so are all children. But what he does now is utterly unbearable."

"Perhaps he dislikes your companion, after all?"

"On no, he certainly likes him!"

"How do you know?"

"Because I asked him."

"In such cases, children often give the wrong answers."

"Nevertheless, he likes him very much. I'll tell you right now why I happen to be so sure of this."

"I am very curious to hear."

"We wanted to marry, my companion and I. But I had decided to marry only if the lad agreed. So I asked him about it, and the boy said to me: 'Mother, you are quite right, at least we will have somebody who earns money for us.' Now you must admit, of course, that he does like his father." (By "father" she means her companion.)

I shake my head and reply: "We shall ask your companion whether he himself is quite convinced that Franz likes him."

The "companion" is called in. He seems a good-natured, attractive person, who looks considerably younger than the woman, between twenty-four and twenty-six years. He too begins right away to describe the unbearable situation with regard to the boy; but one can see from the way he talks that he is quite unhappy in his role of accuser. He speaks touchingly about his efforts on behalf of the boy, and how he plays and studies with him. But he is obviously not aware that his account of the child's behavior goes to prove that the boy definitely rejects him. Only once does he show a glimmer of understanding, when he reports about the incident with the outstretched leg, over which he tripped. He says:

"You know, I have the feeling that the lad did it on purpose; and when a child does such a thing to his father, it is no longer possible to keep him at home."

Thereupon I look up to the woman with a searching glance and remark: "It seems to me that I was right, after all!"

"Sir, what do you mean?" inquires the man immediately.

Then the woman explains to him vividly that according to my opinion Franz does not like him at all.

He replies: "The gentleman cannot be entirely right, but I must admit that sometimes it looks that way." Now he continues, talking to the woman: "This is something we have spoken about so often; the lad behaves in a very strange way and tries to push himself between you and me each time I want to give you a kiss." The woman is visibly startled, and now they begin reminding each other of various tender scenes during with the child's attitude seemed unusual. They are so engrossed in their dialogue that they are unaware of my presence. It is interesting to hear how both of them come more and more to realize that Franz is in fact jealous of his mother's companion.

At this point, I interrupt them by asking the man whether he can tell me why the boy's behavior had deteriorated abruptly just about six weeks ago. He cannot find a reason, although he confirms the fact, which he finds remarkable. I had, of course, a quite definite supposition, but I did not want to state it until I had an appropriate clue. Therefore I ask again, this time addressing the woman: "When did you tell Franz that you intended to marry your companion?" She answers without further thought: "Six weeks ago."

"Don't you notice the coincidence now?"

"Oh, but this is out of the question," she counters with growing dismay, "for I had asked him about it, and he had quite agreed!"

"Yes, of course, he agreed that somebody should earn money to keep both of you; he told you so, but still he does not want to give you up."

I had an interview with Franz also, in the absence of the mother and her companion. From this talk it was clear that the boy disliked the man. This was not surprising: the child had grown up all alone with his mother, until the age of eleven; his real father could not have played any considerable part in his life. Franz therefore enjoyed the most favored position one might imagine. Suddenly there comes along a rival, a stranger who lays claim to his mother. What place in her life this woman accorded her son is evident from the fact that in the question of marrying her companion she made her decision dependent upon the boy's will. The son was not at all inclined to relinquish his good position. As long as the stranger is only a companion who lives in the house, he may be expected to go away one day, as suddenly as he had come. He is agreeable as a playmate, disagreeable because of his fond attentions to the mother. Alternately attracted and repelled, Franz finally develops a perceptible feeling of hatred, once the decision about the marriage was made. He behaves in such a way as to be kicked out; for he feels that if his mother has found herself another man, he himself has nothing more to expect at home. Everything he does shows his wish to get away. Clearest of all is his attitude toward his mother in the case of the welfare allowance, for which he does not get the required signature. It is for his own upbringing that the City of Vienna pays a monthly allowance; this money comes into the family because of the child, it represents his own "earnings."

"If you now love another, let *him* keep you!" This is the unconscious attitude which determines the actions of the child. Therefore he fails to get the signature and his mother does not receive the money which she badly needs while her companion is jobless. In this way the boy shows his mother how necessary he is to her welfare.

Franz was not conscious of the motives of his actions. He had become aware only of his temporary dislike of his mother's companion, and of his present grudge against her; but of course he did not know why he was cross with his mother. His attempt to trip his future stepfather was certainly not intentional, nor was his failure to get the welfare register signed a premeditated action. His was a case of faulty performance, parapraxis, as it is called in psychoanalysis. The things he was doing or not doing, as we had already occasion to remark, were compulsive reactions to the behavior of his mother and her companion. They changed completely after the interview at the child guidance clinic. These plain people had had a poferul experience with me. They now perceived, instinctively rather than through the intellect, that their previous attitude toward the child and the way they had handled him were quite mistaken. At present, they show more understanding and they avoid any particular manifestation of tenderness to each other in the presence of the boy. The mother has restored Franz to that favored position which he enjoyed previously, while the stepfather is content to play the part of an elder friend. But most important of all, they do no longer rail at the child, and they do not watch his actions with distrust as if he were always ready for mischief. Afterwards, the family came to visit me several times, and there is no longer any question of committing Franz to a reform institution.

What we call "education" amounts quite often merely to a release of pent-up emotions on the part of the parents. They are sincerely convinced that they are giving their best to their children; they have not the slightest inkling that their way of treating them is influenced by what they have experienced in their childhood, at the hands of their own parents. If the treatment which they have received in their own day— either loving or rigorous—has been accepted by them as justified, then they will handle their children in quite the same way, without much further thought. If, on the other hand, they have rebelled against the methods of their own upbringing, which they experienced as unjust or condemned as mistaken, then they will handle their children with directly opposite means. Out of their reactions to their childhood training they have developed those rules and standards which now become the basis for the upbringing of their own children. What is usually overlooked is the fact that each child has his own individuality, and that there can be no justification for applying to him rules derived from the experiences of a different personality, even of a parent.

Let us again illustrate this point by a concrete example from our child guidance clinic.

Our welfare worker reports that a twelve-year-old boy who is being brought up by his grandparents is causing them untold difficulties. He is so disobedient that the old folks do not know what to do with him. The school complains about him all the time; he brings back only such homework as his grandfather will do with him; in the classroom he is unbearable, his conduct is disorderly—in one word, he is the *bête noire* of the schoolteacher. Conditions in the family, as described by our welfare worker, are excellent. It is true that the grandparents live very modestly on a limited income, but their little apartment is exceedingly neat and well kept. The way they care for the boy is perfect; he is being treated with the fondest love. The grandparents do everything within their power to bring him up properly, but whatever they do goes wrong. The boy must be provided for in some other way. The municipal welfare board on which I serve decides to take charge.

I invite the grandfather to visit me with his grandchild. He comes, and I take him in before receiving the boy, so as not to hurt the old man's feelings. The impression he makes as he enters my office is that of an old veteran of General Radetzky's days, a square-built frame, not very tall, clean-shaven chin and bushy moustache. This grandfather has exceedingly kind eyes, and he looks like one of the now rare and dying-out specimens of Old Vienna. We have a conversation about his grandchild. In fact, we learn that this is not really his grandson, but the child of an adopted son, whom he and his wife had brought up since infancy. The old man complains about this adopted son, the father of the "grandchild"; he too has gone wrong. Not that he ever committed any crime; but he has been in trouble with the police several times; he is quite wayward and gambles away whatever he earns. The grandfather fears that his present ward, the child of his adopted son, may likewise go astray. But how did it happen that the boy lives with the old folks rather than with his own father? When the boy's father was drafted into the army, he asked grandfather to take charge of the child; and the boy has stayed with him ever since. Anyhow, he is better off that way; otherwise he would have no home at all, as his father leads a quite unsteady life.

It seems remarkable to me that this good old man, who to all appearances is blessed with stolid common sense, has failed twice in succession in bringing up children. Even admitting that his two wards (the adopted son and grandson) did not possess the hereditary predisposition for a normal development, there was still room for some wonderment at his repeated failure and for curiosity about the old man's own experiences in life, which might well provide us with a relevant clue. At least so I thought, and therefore I prodded the grandfather into telling me more about himself and his own youth. It was easy. He liked to dwell on old memories. According to his story, his early years had been exceptionally hard. He was orphaned while still a little child, and had to struggle for bare existence from early boyhood. At the age of ten he earned his keep as a cattle-herd; then a rough village smith taught him his trade; later he wandered all over the world, and it was only in his ripe age that he was able to gain some education through self-instruction, to make up for the schooling which he had never received. I listen gladly to the old man. He talks well, in a picturesque, lively manner. It is as if I were going through his own experiences, and therefore his words sound convincing when finally he says: "I decided when I was still a young man, that if ever I happened to marry, I would give my children a happy youth, for I know what it means to grow up without joy." But he married very late. The couple remained childless. It was a long time before he and his wife found out they could not have children. They were not reconciled to the idea of living without any; so they adopted a child, the father of the boy with whom we are concerned. The old man is still at a loss to explain why this lad, of whom he took care with so much love and who had been given such a nice boyhood, came to nothing, in fact, to the verge of utter ruin. After all the other disappointments in his life, the foster father had to suffer this one too. But I think that we have learned quite enough to perceive much more clearly than the grandfather why his failure was inevitable. If we still have any doubts about it, we need only to observe the old man and his adopted grandchild in a little scene played out in my office. After having talked to the boy alone, I told him in the presence of his grandfather: "I hear that you do your homework only when grandpa works with you. What was the problem in your last assignment?" At this question, the boy turns away from me and looks up at his grandfather. Without showing the least surprise, the old man begins to recite as if he himself were the pupil: "Given two sums of money used as capital, the one of 4,000 shillings and the other of 5,000; the one bearing an annual interest rate of 5 per cent, the other of 4 per cent; and considering that they bear the same total interest—how long was the interest-bearing period in each case?" The grandfather enunciates the problem in the monotone of a schoolboy who stands before his teacher; in his eagerness to help his adopted grandchild he even memorizes the child's lessons for him. The boy need not bother at all, because the old man feels duty-bound to spare him the least effort.

In reaction to his own unhappy childhood the grandfather had developed the compelling urge to provide the adopted children with a joyful and carefree existence. As a result, they became unable to fend for themselves in the struggle for life. Spoiling the child, a natural way to treat a baby, must be kept within bounds as the child grows up, so as to prepare him for the severe demands of reality. But in this case, spoiling was never given up. The grandfather removed every conceivable obstacle from the path of his adopted son and grandson, for no other reason than that he himself had suffered from excessive burdens in his own young days. There was no necessity for his wards to impose upon themselves any restriction of instincts. Yet life was to meet them, inexorably, with its demands, for which they were unprepared. It is clear that at this point they would seek refuge from the unpleasantness of normal life in the gratifications of delinquency. The task of rearing had failed. We may assume that with this particular grandfather any child would grow up to be a misfit. It is of course quite impossible to make him realize why his efforts are doomed to futility: he is much too old for such understanding. If we want to keep the child away from the sorry path followed by his father, we must remove him from the wardship of his adoptive grandparents.

Psychoanalytic psychology has helped us to find out relations and connections which previously remained unnoticed. These first steps into an unexplored region do not yet afford a very deep understanding. That will be gained by further research. Nevertheless, we should recognize that a child's upbringing makes heavy demands upon the parents. It is an exacting task which one cannot always perform through mere good will. Indeed, often enough, it requires also an increased knowledge of the unconscious processes of the psyche.

# VII

## Delinquency in a New Light

A medieval chronicle tells us of a game of five- and six-year-old children, girls and boys, which developed as follows: "And they chose one little boy to be butcher, and another one to be cook, and a third one to be a pig. One little girl was supposed to be another cook and catch the blood of the pig in a dish, so that they could make sausages out of it. According to their plans, the boy who was supposed to be the butcher jumped the boy who was the pig, threw him down, slashed his throat with a knife, and the girl-cook caught the blood. A judge, who happened upon the scene, caught the "butcher" and took him to the courthouse, where the whole council gathered immediately. They were undecided what to do with the boy, assuming that they were dealing with a child criminal. A wise man found the following answer to the predicament, which all the others considered valid:

Paper presented at the Austrian Conference for Community Welfare, Vienna, July, 1948.

*Editor's Note:* The historical pages in this essay were included primarily to indicate to the reader the literature available to Aichhorn when he started out on his life's work. As will be noted, this literature was of scant help to him and contributed nothing significant to the originality and bold departure of his ideas and techniques.

The supreme judge should hold a beautiful red apple in one hand, and a Rhenish goldpiece in the other; then call the boy toward him and hold out both hands. If the boy reached for the apple, he should be pronounced innocent; if he chose the goldpiece, he should be executed. But the child laughingly reached out for the apple." Thus reads the medieval chronicle.

Although a wise man happens upon the scene of a children's gory game, his coming does not dissolve the tension which takes our breath away as we read the story. Finally the child breaks the suspense, because he reaches for the red apple and not for the goldpiece, with which he might have satisfied his greed. In this case, he would have forfeited his life.

For the characterization of medieval concepts, it is immaterial whether this childish game was carried out to its horrible ending, or whether an actual event was greatly exaggerated by frequent telling through the years.

And how do we judge matters today? Though our wayward[1] and criminal juveniles are not subject to capital punishment, we often convict them because they reach out for the goldpiece instead of the apple.

Our lawmakers would consider it absurd if they were asked to reflect on the possibility that unconscious conflicts could be acted out in such a manner that "pretty red apple" and "glittering goldpiece" could be considered as indicative of motives for the deed.

Now, if someone came along who demonstrated that a juvenile by his very nature is not subject to conviction by law, that the juvenile courts represent not the ultimate but only a step which must be followed up by an institution so directed that it evaluates and guides the juvenile, instead of convicting him, such a man would still be considered in many countries today as an impractical idealist, though some other countries might accept his ideas with more benevolence.

[1] *Editor's Note:* In this paper "wayward" is used as Aichhorn used it in *Wayward Youth,* equivalent to juvenile delinquent.

But what would happen to the man who realized that the "apple" and "goldpiece" judgment forces us to assume a different point of view toward the criminal, whether juvenile or adult, and who out of this insight promoted deterrents to crime that differ from the customary?

Inertia is a law pertaining not only to physics. It is applicable generally, but tremendous effort is needed to leave the well-worn tracks of a familiar path and to proceed on a new one.

How does the Penal Code of the Middle Ages look upon the wayward?

At a time when the English hanged a beggar without process of law, after his first relapse; when the French flogged him cruelly "in appropriately growing intensity," cut off or burned off his ears, reserving the gallows for the incorrigible —in those times there existed no special code of law for the wayward. And if in the multitude of small states in Germany beggars were thrown into prison instead of being hanged, this was no demonstration of humane feeling, but, as documented in Krohne's *Prison Report,* it was a matter of expediency, because "if one would have hanged all the vagrants, one would have run out of wood for the gallows and hemp for the ropes."

No attention was paid to the wayward; they were ignored and allowed to drift until they caused too much damage to be overlooked, or until repeated complaints necessitated action by the legal authorities. Then the wayward person was arrested and thrown into prison with other derelict elements, to make him mend his ways by subjecting him to strict discipline and hard labor.

These prisons and workhouses, which originally served only for detention and correction, were used later to house vagrants held under suspicion as well as convicts. From then on the wayward were thrown together not only with vagrants, beggars, vice addicts, and other derelicts, but also with the criminal and the insane—the latter also were incarcerated—all under the same roof, subject to the arbitrary regime of a prison guard or warden. Since the conditions prevailing in those prisons mocked all human dignity, nobody took exception to the custom that the mentally defective and the insane were paraded as a source of amusement before fellow prisoners and visitors.

The idea was to bring to the prisoner the greatest possible amount of suffering through poor accommodations, inadequate food, hard labor, and brutal treatment in word and deed. If through complete neglect of all hygienic facilities the health of the inmates was quickly undermined, the director's conduct of the prisons was gladly condoned.

The law ignored the fact that the prison wardens were in charge of procuring the prison food and special rations, and that consequently the inmates had to put up with the dishonesty of the officers in order not to fall victim to their abuse.

Since no provision was made for separating the sexes in prison, pregnancies frequently occurred, confinements were kept secret and newborn infants killed. The prisoner was exposed to the most sordid aspects of sexuality.

The criminal was not considered a human being like others, but a threat to society, deserving to be treated as such, and if possible to be eliminated.

The Penal Code of Empress Maria Theresia, published in 1768, demonstrates clearly how deeply rooted were the ideas of revenge and intimidation, and how difficult was the transition from corporal and capital punishment to imprisonment. To quote verbatim from the Penal Code of Empress Maria Theresia: "Only small children up to seven years of age, and minors closer to the age of seven than to the age of fourteen are to be exempt from capital punishment through hanging." And still in the year 1832 a nine-year-old child was condemned to death in England because he had broken a store window and stolen 2 pennies worth of paint.

How did individuals and how did society of the Middle Ages look upon the wayward?

The Middle Ages would be misjudged, were we to assume

that public opinion entirely disregarded the dire misery of adult and juvenile prisoners. Awakened during the earliest centuries of Christianity, charitable love for one's fellow man continued. Truly pious people bestowed endowments upon many prisons, in order to help the inmates maintain their morale.

Though it is impossible to enumerate all the achievements since the last quarter of the fifteenth century, both by individuals and by private organizations, a few will be noted here.

Everyone who works in Catholic juvenile welfare organizations is familiar with Hieronymus of Aemiliani (1481-1537) and Joseph of Calasanz (1556-1648). They rescued children roaming the streets, who were alone in the world and exposed to crime: the former during the first half of the sixteenth century after an outbreak of the plague in Venice, the latter during the second half of the sixteenth century in Rome.

St. Vincent de Paul (1576-1660) is considered the most important proponent of Catholic institutional education. He was the first to organize the "Charitable Sisters" into a professional group.

Johannes Baptist de La Salle (1651-1719) was one of the outstanding men who devoted themselves to charitable Catholic institutional education. In 1703 Pope Clemens XI converted a large part of the Hospital San Michele in Rome into an institution for wayward juveniles and delinquents under twenty years of age, for the purpose of "discipline, education, and rehabilitation."

Protestant circles also devoted themselves "for the glory of God" to the salvation of many souls. In 1669 the Protestant councilor Peter Rentzel founded, at his own expense, a spinning mill in Hamburg, to employ the shiftless.

The "Magdalene Service" *(Magdalenenarbeit)* constitutes a chapter all of its own within the framework of welfare organizations for the wayward. Sponsored by Catholics as well as Protestants, it devotes itself to the salvation of youthful prostitutes.

According to the Chronicle of Colmar, in 1226 Rudolph von Worms came upon a number of loitering prostitutes in Colmar and threatened to thrash them with his cane. When they implored him for shelter and food, he was moved to arrange marriage for some of them and helped the others to continue life together in a respectable manner. Before the end of the thirteenth century, fifty convents were established in Germany dedicated to Magdalene Service. The most important foundation grew later into the worldwide organization of the "Ladies of the Good Shepherd." The first Protestant foundation of this kind dates back more than 100 years: in 1836 Fliedner converted the garden house of his parsonage at Kaiserswerth am Rhein into a "Magdalene Foundation" *(Magdalenenstift)*. Obviously the concern for young prostitutes dates far back.

Finally, in the eighteenth century the time was ripe for a revision of the penal laws. The social movement, based on the philosophy of enlightenment, was influenced by a scientific and religious-philanthropic trend. Owing to the influence of the Englishman John Howard and of the Quakers in Pennsylvania, not only was prison reform brought about, but toward the end of the eighteenth century the law was changed: corporal and capital punishment were replaced by imprisonment. The lawgivers recognized that even the criminal has rightful claims on society, that he is a human being like others. From now on, attention is focused on the criminal's personality, and consequently the law views the wayward in a new light.

The first concern of the reformers was not the manner of carrying out sentences, nor the housing of juvenile waywards and criminals, but primarily the question of determining the proper age for becoming subject to the penal laws. The first efforts were devoted to setting this age at an older level. Even though it was felt to be untenable to house wayward and delinquent juveniles and adult criminals together, for a long time these conditions remained unchanged.

In Austria, the initiative was taken relatively early. In 1765, Empress Maria Theresa issued a proclamation ordering the construction of institutions to house only wayward young people. But for another 130 years nothing positive was achieved, due to bickering about who was to foot the bills: the community, the county, or the State, and only on May 24, 1885 an appropriate law was enacted.

It would take many pages to describe the diverse efforts and the serious work required to reach fundamental decisions regarding questions like the following: whether the carrying out of sentences for juveniles required separate institutions, or whether separate areas of general prisons should be used; whether juvenile criminals should be kept strictly separated from the wayward; how penal laws and the carrying out of sentences might gradually be adjusted to the given phase of development in children and juveniles; what obstacles had to be overcome in order to formulate laws establishing preventive care for young people; what efforts were made to establish juvenile welfare laws, etc.

Beginning with the nineteenth century, the reform of penal laws for juveniles and the laws for juvenile welfare widened the scope for private juvenile welfare organizations, and gave them new impetus. Improper conditions were to be corrected both in institutions and in foster homes, and educational organizations were founded to pursue this goal.

The first educational organization was founded in Germany by the Protestant minister Brau in Neunkirchen near Moers; it became the model for over 100 similar organizations. The first Catholic educational organization was founded in Muenster, Westfalen, in 1848. The most successful of these organizations and the one with the widest scope is the "Serapic Work of Love" *(Seraphische Liebeswerk).* Also to be included is the St. Johannis Organization, founded by Maximilian I of Bavaria, which has both Catholic and Protestant sections. These were the beginnings of the later juvenile welfare organizations.

A new epoch began with the work of Heinrich Pestalozzi, who rose to prominence in Switzerland. We need not en-

large on his international fame. He pointed the way for
Jacob Wehrli (Wehrli Schools) and Heinrich Zeller, who
founded a three-year training school for directors of institutions, and who contributed important ideas toward the development of the future salvation home movement *(Rettungs-
hauswesen).*

The Protestant salvation home movement of Germany
furnished institutional training with the effective impetus to
try to approximate educational situations as they exist within
the family. Johannes Falk in Weimar, Graf Adelbert von der
Recke Volmerstein, and especially Johann Heinrich Wichern,
whose work shines like a beacon in the whole field—all of
them played an integral part in the beginning and the
development of "salvation home work."

"The "Rauhes Haus" in Hamburg is not only the model
of more than 400 institutions in Germany, but Wichern himself is the guiding spirit who trains young men as counselors to the children in order to become educators themselves. He refers to his training school as "the core of
the whole."

Fliedner, whom I mentioned earlier in connection with
Magdalene work, founded the Home for Deaconesses.
Eventually, more than sixty similar homes sprang up all
over the world, as well as twelve homes for men. The
deaconesses and deacons constitute the largest number of
educators, house fathers, and house mothers within the
Protestant juvenile welfare organizations.

Everyone who studies the history of the welfare movement
in all its ramifications cannot help being amazed, and must
realize the insignificance of his own contributions. There have
been magnificent achievements, some out of naïve motiva-
tions, others out of true love for one's fellow man, out of guilt
feelings, and a variety of other reasons. The history of the
welfare movement also reflects the ups and downs of the
times: upswings in times of general prosperity, and low ebbs
during wars and general depressions. And especially in times
of need do we find individuals emerging from all classes of

society who fight to preserve what has been gained and to
help the welfare movement reach new goals.

But the student of history will also recognize that welfare
work was born out of deeply felt religious obligation, out of
a charitable impulse, which developed into social insight and
the understanding that the troubled child has the right to
be helped. And finally there is the economic principle to be
considered: preventing crime costs less than fighting crime.
How does science consider the wayward?

The penal laws established toward the end of the nineteenth century focused on the personality of the criminal,
and this new attitude opened the way for science to make
the criminal and the wayward subjects of research. And yet,
science was slow in taking interest in this problem. Only
from 1876 do the natural sciences begin to concern themselves with the criminal, but not for a long time to come do
they take notice of the wayward. "It is hard to believe,"
comments the *Encyclopaedia Brittannica*, "that until the publication of Lombroso's *The Criminal Personality* there had
never been a serious scientific attempt to study the criminal."

Lombroso's concept of the "born criminal" is based on
precise body and skull measurements. For a long time research proceeded along these lines (Ferri, Kurella, Kretsch-
mer, et al.). Criminal anthropology and criminal psychology
limited themselves to the study of endogenous and exogenous components leading to crime, even though Lombroso
himself, spurred on by adversaries and followers alike, modified his earlier findings and stressed environmental factors
in his later work.

Criminal psychology first began to appear about 1800; the
criminologist Gross from Graz can be considered its founder.
Its earliest studies concerned endogenous causes of criminality. The second stage was initiated by Karl Kraus, who directed his research to environment.

Even the classic students of the wayward, Gruhle (1907)
and Gregor Voigtländer (1918), base their inquiries on statistical methods and try to explain the factors leading to

waywardness by the influence of inborn disposition (Anlage) and environment.

Aschaffenburg works in the same direction, including among endogenous causes the seasons, scene of the crime, race, religion, etc. But he comes closer to our own interpretation when he says in his critical view of Lombroso: "Criminals are not, as Lombroso believed, born criminals, but have become criminals. This is due to the fact that there exists a disharmony between their character and the demands of the life which they are required to lead."

Scientific psychiatry defined its position in regard to the criminal and the wayward comparatively late. The results of psychiatric research are of prime importance to welfare educators: psychiatry gives us diagnoses and furnishes the concept of psychopathy, though the latter is still controversial. It has pointed out the influence of mental deficiency, hysteria, and epileptic states of semi-consciousness as causes for crime and waywardness; all this is of significance in determining the question of guilt.

Birnbaum (1914) in his monograph on the psychopathic criminal goes so far as to declare: "Whoever has learned to recognize the psychopath correctly in the course of criminal trials and in the carrying out of sentences has not only explored pathological criminality, but to a certain degree understands criminality altogether."

The biology of crime came into consideration between 1920 and 1930. It attempts to combine criminal anthropology, criminal psychopathology, and criminal psychology. Lenz laid its systematic foundations. His concept of criminal biology appears new and valuable because he deals with the fundamental problem in a broad biopsychological manner. The basic problem is the essence and development of the criminal personality. His approach incorporates knowledge of modern psychology, psychopathology, genetics, and hereditary biology. Lenz methodically investigates hereditary factors and life history, and on the basis of his research arrives at the following conclusion: "If the forces of the drives or certain emotional constellations of the moment tip the balance, then we are dealing with the endogenous criminal." On the other hand, we see the criminal deed as exogenous crime, precipitated mainly through stimuli of the environment.

In this context Franz Exner and others should also be mentioned. There is an extensive bibliography in this field. In 1912, Gruhle refers to the basic literature on welfare as "staggering." A paper by Ilse Schulze-Steinen in 1935 titled "German Research into the Causes for Juvenile Waywardness during the Last Thirty Years" enumerates fifty authors with sixty-five publications as well as dictionaries and handbooks. In 1944, as supplement V of the Swiss Journal of Psychology there appeared a paper, "Psychology of Waywardness" by E. Rutishauser, Director of the Juvenile Authorities of the Kanton Aargau. Among the 105 authors cited, he included a number who are oriented toward depth psychology. He differs markedly from many others, since he considers the etiology, degree, and extent of waywardness as a reaction to consciously experienced displeasure; in this he approaches most closely our own views.

Now the question arises whether it is expedient to look at waywardness from still a different angle.

Educators are motivated by the need to be helpful. The juvenile laws set the framework for our endeavors. We call on science for assistance in our work.

What has science given us so far? The diagnosis, which justifies commitment to institutional care; yet this diagnosis circumscribes the limits of our work often quite narrowly. Though the diagnosis gives us valuable information, it sometimes shakes our confidence, because it may undermine our positive attitude, our faith in the success of our work.

But what neither criminal anthropology, criminal psychology, nor criminal biology or psychiatry can give us, is this: insight into the dynamics of the etiology of waywardness; enlightenment into the psychic play of forces that led to the condition which the educator has to set straight in order to achieve rehabilitation.

Let us start out with some very simple reflections. Whenever institutional education of the wayward is discussed, one hears that the best organization, the most generous funds, the most lavishly furnished rooms are of no avail if the right educators are lacking.

Experience has taught us that there are personalities capable of rehabilitating the wayward. In fact, such people have always existed, long before science ever concerned itself with the wayward, and such people will always exist, even without the benefit of science.

If it is true the personality of the educator is significant in the rehabilitation of the wayward, then we are prompted to ask: what is the nature of this educating force? Perhaps here is the place to leave the beaten path and set out in a new direction.

Scrutiny of the personalities of those talented in this field reveals that all of them have the capacity to win the trust and affection of their charges quickly and easily, and that thus the first step toward rehabilitation is taken.

Why are some people capable of establishing this contact, and others not?

Understanding the wayward does not mean groping to find inborn defects and damage caused by environment. The delinquent is not just the sum of reactions of endogenous components or exogenous ones. He is unique, and in order to understand him we must assess his present personality correctly, at first by intuition.

Whoever wants to work successfully with young delinquents has to be capable of stepping out of his own secure position in the social community, to identify himself with the offender, and thereby to become receptive to and understanding of the intricacies of the delinquent's character structure.

If, however, the educator remains reserved and identified with society, and feels protective of the laws which the wayward youth is violating, no meaningful contact can be established. Since the wayward youth remains a stranger to him, the educator will unintentionally assume the role of defender of society rather than bend his efforts toward true rehabilitation of the delinquent.

The wayward individual experiences these efforts as coercion to make him relinquish his innate personality and so he fights back. When the educator tries to persuade the delinquent gently and benevolently to give up his subjective personality voluntarily, he sees his efforts fail, and then he often gives up this approach and resorts to violence.

In the beginning phase of rehabilitation it matters not how society views the delinquent and to what extent he considered a disturbing outsider. Of crucial importance is the need to learn how the wayward youth himself experiences society. Often he fights a singlehanded battle against society as a rebel who resents all demands for conformity as an unnatural deprivation of his freedom. Often the wayward still preserves in his ego traits characteristic of primitive man, who rejects demands for social integration as the worst injustice imposed on him.

But while it is of prime importance that the educator identify with the wayward youth in the beginning phase of rehabilitation, it would be dangerous for him to persist in this attitude, since that would mean becoming wayward himself. If identification is followed by a second phase of viewing the delinquent objectively, the educator will have learned to assess the wayward youth correctly and it becomes possible to find the right path toward rehabilitation. Even though he will have to exact a sacrifice from the wayward, the educator will now proceed without resorting to misdirected humanitarianism, in recognition of the fact that the wayward youth can but act in his own interest, rather than under pressure of a morally superior society.

How does the educator find the "right approach"? By focusing his interest primarily on the early childhood of the delinquent, and by directing his powers of observation and examination toward the first community in which the child lives, the family. He will note immediately that within the family the interpersonal relationships are of unique kind and intensity, which will never appear in quite the same way in any other organization of society.

He finds, furthermore, that as long as these relationships are not disturbed, as long as the interfamilial libidinal balance remains intact, the children develop normally. He will also find that the libidinal balance may be disturbed not only by the member who later on becomes wayward, but also by any other member of the family, as well as by outside circumstances. Obviously, endogenous as well as exogenous factors play a role.

Assessing the wayward properly does not entail establishing statistically how many endogenous and exogenous components led to the disturbance, but to learn how it came about that certain factors contributed to the development of just that particular personality which confronts us.

One of the causes of waywardness is without doubt a disturbance of the libidinal balance: the need for love satisfied either too little or too much; being shut out of the community or overly involved in it.

The second cause refers to the superego. Man cannot live without guiding principles. During childhood the adults concerned with his rearing furnish the guidance, and from the end of childhood until death the superego guides the personality. This superego, as psychoanalysis calls the inner authority, this critical arbiter that judges the ego, approves or condemns, is not present from the beginning of life, but develops gradually. At first the environment guides the child with demands and prohibitions. As the child identifies himself with those who rear him, their standards become part of his ego and are internalized as inner authority or superego.

The stronger the affectionate relationships are, the stronger is the tendency toward identification. Children form the most tender relationships with their parents, and therefore the nucleus of the superego is formed in the nursery. All later identifications, with teachers, religious leaders, characters in literature, etc., form layers around this nucleus.

The nucleus of the superego will not develop if children are deprived of needed love. This happens when parents pay little attention to their children, neglect them, or are indifferent to them. It happens when children are shuttled early in life from one foster home to another, as is the case with public dependents, where children do not have time to develop feelings of affection toward foster parents and to identify with them. Such children absorb all later identifications as loose structures that do not really take hold. Their superego is an unreliable guide; they consequently have a labile attitude toward all demands of society. Many wayward symptoms are thus explained, and they are amenable to cure through correct re-education.

Children take over into the superego not only their parents' orders and prohibitions, but also their general attitudes toward life, toward nonpersonal matters, religion, ethics, morals, and the values which the parents attach to ideas and to material goods.

If the parents' orientation coincides with the ideals of society and if they live harmoniously within the community, then this attitude becomes by the process of identification part of the children's superego. If, however, the parents are at variance with the community—for example, if they are antisocial in a social culture, materialistic in an idealistically oriented one, antireligious in a religious one—then their children will be reacted against by the community as outsiders, will meet with difficulties, be judged as wayward, even though they act only according to the dictates of their superegos.

If one of the parents is himself delinquent or wayward, then in the process of identification traits of waywardness will enter into the formation of the child's superego. In this case also, certain forms of waywardness result from a labile orientation toward society.

A child is bound to become totally antisocial when he is brought up in a family of criminals and takes over their values. Many wayward children of this kind come before the juvenile courts. They do not understand the judge and he does not understand them, because the judge and the wayward live in worlds totally opposed to each other.

But waywardness results not only from disturbed libidinal balance or a warped superego. Waywardness may also result from a conflict between the three psychic systems within the total personality: the "ego", the "id," and the "superego." If an overly powerful superego throttles the infantile instinctual drives storming up from the id, then, depending on circumstances, either a neurosis or neurotic waywardness will result. If the id overwhelms the ego, the result is not necessarily one of the familiar perversions, though there exists waywardness which is the equivalent of a perversion. When the ego is overwhelmed by the id and regression results, this condition does not always lead to psychosis, but (again given certain conditions) may result in the psychotic wayward, the psychotic criminal.

This form of waywardness is encountered relatively seldom in welfare education, because this type passes into crime within a short time. These juveniles almost always end up in institutions for criminals, where they pose a tremendous problem. It is almost hopeless to attempt their rehabilitation without psychoanalytic treatment.

In the etiology of waywardness, not only the content but also the form of the superego are important. It is by no means unimportant whether the superego demands compliance with its dictates brutally, or whether it awaits fulfillment of its dictates hesitatingly, admonishingly, or imploringly.

Since the form of the superego also stems from identification with the parents, the investigator of the wayward youth has to explore the manner in which the parents demand compliance with rules that suppress instinctual drives: whether this occurs in a forceful, brutal, weak, or expectant manner. How can the superego develop into a reliable guide if the parents do not agree on methods of training; if the mother is permissive when the father is demanding, or the other way around? The child identifies himself with both. The end result is often a wayward child, living with the feeling: "Nothing can happen to me."

These briefly suggested etiological considerations demonstrate clearly that waywardness begins at a very young age, sometimes in earliest childhood, long before it becomes noticeable to the outside world. Twenty-five years ago I suggested the use of the term "phase of latent delinquency" to designate that span of time in which the mechanisms of waywardness are formed, but no symptoms are as yet noticeable. The slightest impetus may then change the latent into the manifest phase with evident symptoms.

We have to differentiate between the cause and the precipitant of waywardness.

I repeat: There are two phases of waywardness: the latent and the manifest, i.e., the phase without symptoms and the phase with symptoms. Treating delinquency does not mean eliminating the symptoms, returning manifest waywardness to the former stage of latent waywardness, so often accomplished through conviction in court. Rehabilitating the wayward means uncovering the causes which brought about the latent condition, and removal of these causes.

All these reflections and many others which constantly come to mind in rehabilitation work force us to the conclusion that with the help of psychoanalysis a new way opens up to get to the root of our problems. This will be accomplished by those who come after me and agree with my approach. I myself shall not proceed beyond the preliminary work.

When this task is accomplished, then the total chaos that waywardness presents to us today will be disentangled. Juvenile welfare authorities and welfare educators will then not be confronted with an endless confusion of damaged juveniles and in desperation yield to the temptation to join with society and the law in condemning them. As a logical result of scientific research, we will be equipped with knowledge of symptomatology, etiology, and therapy of waywardness.

The rehabilitation of the wayward will no longer be limited to the accidental success of gifted educators, but will be the predictable result of systematic scientific work.

# BIBLIOGRAPHY

AICHHORN, A. (1925), *Verwahrloste Jugend*. Vienna: Internationaler psychoanalytischer Verlag. *Wayward Youth.* New York: Viking Press, 1935; New York: Meridian Books. 1955.

—— (1932), Erziehungsberatung [Child Guidance]. *Zeitschrift für psychoanalytische Pädagogik*, 6:445-488.

ALTMANN, S. (1929), Das Jugendgerichtgesetz [The Law Establishing Juvenile Courts]. *Handausgabe Österreich, Gesetze und Verordnungen*, Heft 244. Vienna: Österreichische Staatsdruckerei.

ASCHAFFENBURG, G. (1923), *Das Verbrechen und seine Bekämpfung*. Heidelberg: Winter.

BIRNBAUM, K. (1914), *Die psychopathischen Verbrecher*. Berlin: Langenscheidt.

FREUD, S. (1914), On Narcissism: An Introduction. *Collected Papers*, 4. London: Hogarth Press, 1950.

—— (1920), Beyond the Pleasure Principle. *Standard Edition*, 18. London; Hogarth Press, 1955.

---

*Editor's Note:* As the interested reader may have observed, the appended bibliography does not always correspond to specific quotes in Aichhorn's text, but reflects his general reading in the field of juvenile delinquency.

—— (1921), Group Psychology and the Analysis of the Ego. *Standard Edition*, 18. London: Hogarth Press, 1955.

GREGOR, A. (1918), *Die Verwahrlosung*. Berlin: Karger.

GRUHLE, H. W. (1912), *Die Ursachen der Jugendlichenverwahrlosung und Kriminalität*. Berlin: Springer.

KRAEPELIN, E. (1908), *Lehrbuch der Psychiatrie*. Leipzig: Barth.

LAZAR, E. (1920), Heilspädagogische Gruppierung in einer Anstalt für verwahrloste Kinder. *Zeitschrift für Kinderheilkunde*, 27, Heft 1-2.

LENZ, F. (1923), In: *Grundriss der menschlichen Erblichkeitslehre*, by E. Baur, E. Fischer, & F. Lenz. München: Lehmann.

RANK, O. (1912), *Das Inzestmotiv in Dichtung und Sage*. Leipzig: Deuticke.

SEIFERT, E. (1912), *Psychiatriche Undersuchungen über Fürsorgezöglinge*. Halle: Marhold.

# Index